SIR IAIN HALL

GLASS CEILINGS

ENHANCING SOCIAL MOBILITY – LEADERSHIP LESSONS FROM CHARTER SCHOOLS

First Published 2018

by John Catt Educational Ltd,
12 Deben Mill Business Centre, Old Maltings Approach,
Melton, Woodbridge IP12 1BL

Tel: +44 (0) 1394 389850 Fax: +44 (0) 1394 386893
Email: enquiries@johncatt.com
Website: www.johncatt.com

ISBN: 978 1 909717 59 1

Set and designed by John Catt Educational Limited

Contents

This book is dedicated to those school leaders and teachers who work tirelessly in helping the young people in their schools break through the glass ceilings that restrict their social mobility

I would like to thank Peter Gaul for his patience and helpful suggestions in checking the early drafts, Katie Sharp for help before going to print and Shane Ierston, Andrew Reay, Mark O'Hagan and Peter Gaul for successfully leading their schools in delivering the vision outlined in this book.

"If you want to see the poor remain poor, generation after generation, just keep the standards low in their schools and make excuses for their academic shortcomings and personal misbehaviour. But please don't congratulate yourself on your compassion."

Thomas Sowell
American economist and philosopher
Creators Syndicate 2000.01.15

Prologue:
Doubts and Reflections

October 2010:
O'Hare Airport, Chicago

There must be a time in each of our lives when we suddenly think 'I might have just got things a little wrong'. This happened to me on a cold Sunday night in October 2010, while waiting for a 'red-eye' flight from Chicago to Manchester, having just led my fourth Future Leader's study tour of a party of North West aspirant school leaders on a trip to see some of the best charter schools in the city. The group had dispersed among the many shops in O'Hare Airport, looking for last minute souvenirs, while I nursed a coffee in a deserted Starbucks. I had been a headteacher for some 23 years and thought that I'd had a successful career but what I had seen on my latest trip confirmed my growing doubts that we might have the wrong approach to urban education back in the UK.

Many questions were swirling in my head. Why were the urban schools I had visited in the US so successful at getting their students into the country's leading colleges and universities? Why were we seeing so few students from challenging urban areas in England accessing our leading universities? Why were so many of the places that these universities had to offer taken up by students from the independent sector? Why do these students gain almost 50% of the 'A' grades awarded each year when they only account for 15% of the entries? Why are so many state schools not able to replicate such levels of success? Gaining straight 'A's might be a mountain to climb for a student living in a challenging urban area but such a result could open many doors to a prosperous future. Almost 80% of our leading judges and barristers and 50% of our leading medics, scientists and journalists have all followed the Oxbridge route to a successful career. What was stopping our urban youngsters accessing these glittering prizes? What were the fees being charged in the independent sector buying that could not be freely available in the state sector? Most of the people I have met who have been educated in the independent sector often seemed to be more rounded, confident individuals, always ready to grasp the opportunities and challenges that are presented to them. How did they gain such confidence? Was it a class difference? Was it the social circles they mixed in? Was it the curriculum they were following in school? Was it the level of challenge they faced in their school? Whatever it was, it enabled them to gain a disproportionate number of places that were on offer in our leading universities and this imbalance was limiting the access chances of young people who were growing up in challenging urban areas. This lack of access was forming an almost impenetrable glass ceiling to their social mobility.

I accept that there is much at fault with the selection processes used by many universities and that they could be admitting more students from state schools, especially those serving challenging urban areas, but this still does not explain why 50% of the top grades are achieved by students from the independent sector. If this glass ceiling is to be permanently broken, then we, as educators in the state system, need to discover the DNA of the best schools, state and independent, and emulate them. Failure to do so would mean allowing this social injustice to continue. High-quality education and equality of opportunity has to be a civil right for all, and not be limited to the more financially advantaged in our society.

2010 had been a year of turmoil in the educational world. In May, the Conservative Party, led by David Cameron, defeated Gordon Brown's Labour Party in the general election but did not have a substantial majority and could not form a government. After prolonged discussions, the Conservatives agreed to form a coalition government with the Liberal Democrats. The original Conservative manifesto had promised to import school reforms that 'have worked so well in countries like the USA, Canada and Sweden'. Once the ink was dry on the coalition agreement, Michael Gove was appointed Education Secretary at the renamed Department for Education. An Academies Act was rushed through parliament, allowing existing schools to convert to academy status and permitting new providers to open American-style charter schools, which were to be known as 'free schools'. Why the sudden charge? Michael Gove and his researchers had obviously observed exactly the same evidence that I had spent four years observing on Future Leaders' study tours. Some charter schools, released from central control, were producing incredible results in challenging and highly deprived urban areas, where previously there had only been educational failure, resulting in high levels of student dropout rates and disillusionment with education as a whole. Not every charter school was highly successful but, if we were to improve urban education, then the challenge would be to understand what the successful schools were doing that made them so special? To unlock the answer, you have to understand the history as to why they were created.

The concept of the charter school was not new. The idea was first muted by Ray Budde, a professor at the University of Massachusetts, in 1974. Unfortunately, it never really gathered support until the early 1990s when a small group of educators and policymakers came together to develop a charter school model. The core of the model was the belief that public schools, and not the state or district, would be held accountable for student learning. In exchange for this autonomy, school leaders would be given freedom to do whatever it takes to help students achieve, and would share the successful outcomes with the broader public school system so that all students benefit. They would still be publicly funded, but would be governed by their own unique 'charter', approved by the state and not subject to regular public school regulations. This 'charter' would have to explicitly define the proposed schools' goals and provide a framework for measuring success. An important feature of each charter was an agreement that each school would be personally accountable for student progress and achievement rather than the district or state. Failure to demonstrate success would result in the removal of the charter and the closure of the school. While the state or district retained these powers, the school would assume responsibility for everything else, therefore producing autonomous, self-accountable schools within a wider state system.

Minnesota's legislature passed the first charter law in 1991, and the first charter school opened in 1992. It was unique in that it only offered places to students from low-income families and was initially designed to accommodate students who had dropped out of mainstream education. Most of these young people came from homes that were wrecked through poverty or drug abuse. School records from 1992 show that some 25% of its intake in the first year were homeless and all of the 35 students who attended had a history of truancy or other disciplinary problems. In the spring of 1993, 17 of those students graduated to high school. The secret of the school's success was the deep belief of its founders that, irrespective of educational starting points or previous track record, these youngsters had potential and you just had to get them believing in themselves.

For me, this was the first piece in the jigsaw. I had spent years working with dedicated teachers in preparing young people for external examinations and, although we continually encouraged them to believe they could be successful, we never deliberately honed those character traits in them that would make this happen. We never deliberately exposed them, from an early age, to character-building experiences that would give them the aspiration, determination, tenacity and resilience to break through the glass ceiling. Perhaps we had been using the wrong approaches.

Part 1:
The Early Years of Headship

1980–89: The Start of my Leadership Journey

My leadership journey to O'Hare Airport began in 1980 when, at the far too young age of 37, I gained my first headship and was charged with bringing two struggling schools in inner-city Liverpool together onto one site. The schools, John Hamilton High School and Lambeth Secondary Modern, had been fairly popular and successful in their day, but had gone into decline and were struggling to attract pupil numbers. One of the two had to close if a non-faith school was to be maintained in the area.

It was the first headship that I had applied for and I had no idea of the form that the interview would take. In retrospect, it was a process that would never happen today. I arrived at the grounds of John Hamilton School some 30 minutes early and sat in my car watching the pupils straggle in. Uniform was poor, there were many harmless scuffles at the gate and smoking was prevalent among the older pupils who stubbed their cigarettes out at the school gates. I began doubting the wisdom of applying but decided to persevere and gain 'interview experience'.

The shortlisted applicants were gathered together at 9am in the school dining room. There were eight of us and I was by far the youngest candidate. After a few words from the school's adviser we were given a whistle-stop tour of the school that, we were told, was to become the permanent site. We never met any of the current staff and were kept well away from the students. Most of our questions were met by a stock response of 'Well that will be up to you – if you are appointed'. The school had yet to be given a name; the new head would be expected to draw up a staffing structure within 48 hours of being appointed, without knowing the names or talents of the teachers at either school. Job descriptions would need to be produced to support the staffing structure and existing staff would be expected to apply for posts on the new structure before the end of the month. My previous posts had not given me the experience that was obviously required to successfully achieve these goals and, as there were three current headteachers in the group of applicants, it was highly unlikely that I would be appointed, so I decided to relax and treat the day as a learning experience.

After the whistle-stop tour, we were then whisked to the city's education offices to be interviewed by a panel of 12 politicians and the chief education officer. The interview was bizarre and I am glad that we are now much more refined in appointing school leaders. It was held in a large room and the 13-person panel sat around a beautiful circular table. The process commenced with the chief education officer taking me through my CV and that was probably the nearest we came to discussing my ability to merge two schools. Each member of the panel had an obligatory question to ask me, with the opening question being to describe my leadership style. I know that I waffled my way through the answer nervously, throwing in as many buzzwords as I could remember. Each member of the panel then asked a question and we slowly worked our way around the table. The questions reflected the interests of each individual member of the panel and had little to do with the challenges that would face the successful candidate or the new school. I was asked my opinion on the use of prefects to do duties while the staff sat in their rooms drinking tea; what was my opinion of the quality of school meals; did I believe in corporal punishment; did I support Liverpool or Everton, what newspaper did I read and if it was the salary that encouraged me to apply. I began to realise, in answering these questions, that diplomacy was a well-desired trait for successful headship. Throughout the interview one of the politicians never stopped reading the Daily Mirror and, when it was his turn to ask a question, he asked the same one as a previous member of the panel! I was not impressed by the process and was relieved when it was over. Afterwards, I was allowed to rejoin the other applicants, who were sat in silence in a neighbouring anteroom.

My second learning experience that day was that the ability to withstand tedium was another preferred trait for successful headship. The actual interviews took almost six hours and we were not offered lunch, but could leave the building to visit a nearby sandwich shop. After we had been interviewed, we all started to relax and laughed at some of the questions we had been asked. The existing heads seemed very confident and it was with jaw-dropping surprise that, shortly after 5pm, I was asked to rejoin the panel, where I was offered the headship, 'despite my age' as the chair commented. With a heavy mixture of excitement, fear and trepidation, I nodded my head and accepted the post. Having shaken a few hands, I stumbled out of the education offices and found a bench to sit on as I wondered, 'why me?' and 'how on earth am I going to face up to the challenge'?

Reflecting back, more than 30 years later, I still wonder how the panel came to its decision. Today's panel would not simply be asking each candidate about their leadership style, but would delve much deeper through a series of well-planned exercises designed to explore each candidate's vision for the school, as well as their courage and determination to achieve their vision. It would be looking for a candidate who had a genuine passion for teaching and learning. Emotional intelligence would figure highly on their list of requirements, as they sought someone with the ability to foster good relationships throughout the school as well as the ability to build and empower successful teams. It would need to see which candidate had a good sense of judgement in order to make crucial decisions, as well as the determination and resilience to carry those decisions out. Above all, the panel would be seeking a good and warm communicator who had the ability to persuade staff to go the extra mile in seeking success for the students. Leadership development has come a long way since 1980 and our schools are better for it.

Over the next few months my amazement at being appointed gave way to a growing sense of excitement at the challenges that lay ahead. The 'new' school was to be housed on the campus of John Hamilton High School and would be called Breckfield Community School. The school was situated in one of the most deprived and toughest areas of the city. There were several local gangs that regularly challenged each other in turf wars. It was an all-white area, with the school building being adjacent to the headquarters of the Liverpool branch of the Orange Lodge. The Orange Order is a long-standing Protestant organisation, primarily based in Northern Ireland, that was named after the Dutch-born king, William of Orange. There was a fierce historical community loyalty to the lodge, which was further fuelled by the ongoing Troubles in Northern Ireland. Each year, on the 12th of July, I discovered that the school would empty as families joined the annual march to Southport. There were some things far more important to the community than education!

Prior to the amalgamation, John Hamilton High had a reputation of being a 'tough' school. Discipline was kept by a frequent and rigorous adherence to the use of the cane. The 'punishment book' I inherited showed little mercy, with daily beatings to both boys and girls. Lambeth Secondary Modern School was the complete opposite with little use of the cane and a strong supportive pastoral system.

The staff of both schools were against the amalgamation. They were angry that their efforts in bringing stability to the lives of some of the most troubled youngsters in the city had not been recognised. They felt that they were being treated as 'failures' because local birth rates had declined. Morale was low and, in our first staff meeting, they sat in two distinct camps at either side of the school hall. Each group thought that they had established the 'right' school ethos in their own school – prior to the amalgamation – and that the new school should simply adopt this ethos. After addressing the meeting and delivering what I thought was a pretty decent 'Agincourt' speech, I asked if there were any questions. There was only one question – when would the new staffing structure be published? People were quite rightly worried about their futures. Having had to draw up the new structure, I was not the most popular of people, as rivals were pitched against each other in trying to hang on to their original status. This was not the positive start that I was naturally seeking. I had discovered a new stage to Tuckman's team building model, in that understandable emotional turmoil preceded forming, norming, storming and performing.

The future prospects of the new school, which was to be called Breckfield Community School, did not look promising. The projected intake of new students was, according to the local authority, to be 180. Most year groups above Year 7 just about met that target as we brought the two school populations together but, unfortunately, when we opened the doors in September only 58 prospective Year 7 pupils walked through them. Being 122 students short of the target, I began to understand that making the amalgamation successful was going to be a tough struggle for a young, inexperienced headteacher.

Somehow, I had managed to convince the staff that our biggest enemies were closure and redundancy and that we were all in the same boat. Using these joint threats as our 'burning platform', we were soon united in our purpose to prove to the whole of the city that we were going to become a school to be reckoned with. Once the difficulties of the restructure had been overcome and the new school year was underway, the staff started to come together and worked tirelessly in bringing about root-and-branch change. Corporal punishment was replaced by a rewards-based culture. Classrooms became focused more on academic success than containment and a strong pastoral system, consisting of extremely dedicated teachers who fully recognised the problems of growing up in challenging urban areas, drove up attendance, improved behaviour and allowed teachers to teach, with little interruption.

We soon made contact with local primary school headteachers and began to develop many inter-primary competitions that were based, for obvious reasons, on the Breckfield site. We needed to get these young pupils and their parents used to coming in to the local secondary school. Within three years we were recognised by the Department for Education (DfE) as having a highly successful primary liaison programme and, by 1985, the school was oversubscribed, with steadily, but slowly, increasing academic outcomes. We had developed a thriving community outreach programme and over 800 people attended our adult education classes each week. Despite still struggling with academic outcomes, we were recognised as being a beacon of good urban practice and were invited by the Northern Ireland Office to partner with a group of Belfast headteachers as they started to refocus their schools and work in partnership, despite the ongoing Troubles.

Sadly, it was not success and happiness every day. Like all schools, there were highs and lows on the road to recovery. One of the lowest moments was being greeted, on arrival one Monday morning, with the news that one of our senior students had died over the weekend after attending a party. The whole school was in shock. I contacted the family to offer our condolences and support after such a tragic event. When the date of the funeral was announced, a group of parents asked me if I would close the school as a mark of respect. Patiently and carefully, but much to their disappointment, I explained that I couldn't. They were not impressed. However, I had arranged with Godfrey Butland, the local vicar, for some pupils, myself and a few staff members who had known the young girl well to attend the funeral. By 9am on the day it was to take place, we realised that we were going to have mass absenteeism. I rang Godfrey immediately and told him to expect a large congregation. He said he would keep two rows of seats for the staff. We gathered all of the students who had turned up for school in the assembly hall and, leaving them with a few teachers, as many staff as we could release walked around the corner to the church for the service. All of our 'truants' were either in the church or lining the pathway to wait for the hearse. As we walked down the aisle to the pews Godfrey had kept for us, the parents and students inside the church started to applaud our arrival. The community's response to their teachers' attendance was a true sign of respect and gratitude.

Another bad Monday was when I arrived at school to discover that someone had broken into the technology department and stolen all of the woodworking tools. Burglary was a fact of life in challenging urban areas but this was quite catastrophic as the Certificate of Secondary Education practical examination in woodwork was to take place on the Thursday. While the school office set about contacting other schools to ask if we could borrow some tools (we were not yet in the era of cheque book management and had no way of purchasing new ones before Thursday) I wrote a letter to all parents pleading for information so that we could get the tools back and proceed with the examination. Early on Wednesday morning, a man arrived at the school asking to see me 'privately'. Sat in my office, he told me that he lived on the local estate and, because his 'bad back' prevented him from working, he acted as an unpaid social worker on the estate. He said that he had discovered who had stolen the tools and that nobody would ever 'grass them up', but he was confident he could buy the tools back off them. When I asked how much he replied that he could probably get them for £50. Knowing that I could not use school funds, I naively agreed to meet him later that afternoon after I had been to the bank. However, I told him that I would not be handing over any money until we had the tools. After he left, I headed straight to the bank to withdraw £50 from my account. That afternoon he returned with a large canvas bag containing tools. He said that he had managed to get most of them back so I handed the money over, relieved that the examination could proceed.

After he had left, I rang the local police to speak to my community officer and told him that we had managed to get most of the tools back. He asked me to describe the unofficial social worker and, on hearing the description, he said that he knew him and would pay him a visit. On the Thursday morning the local station said that they had recovered my money but I needed to call in and make a statement. It would appear that the police had raided my informant's home the night before and found the rest of the tools, as well as my £50. He was arrested but, in his statement admitting the offence, he accused me of receiving stolen goods! Fortunately the police sorted it out, but for the remainder of the week my leadership colleagues took to calling me Fagin!

The staff performed magnificently in the nine years I worked alongside them and the success of the school was their success. My first headship had been a really satisfying experience but I was conscious that I'd had a fair amount of 'beginner's luck'. My biggest failing, in retrospect, was that I had not improved academic outcomes as much as I would have liked. I'd had too much of a focus on caring rather than pushing our students academically. Why had I taken this stance in my first headship? The school served one of the poorest areas in the city. Unemployment was exceptionally high and finding the money to live from day to day was an accepted way of life. Crime was rife and the lure of the gang was a formidable foe for schools to face. Many children lived in unstructured families and arrived at school tired, after late nights watching too much television, and hungry, having skipped breakfast.

In his famous 'Ruskin' speech, the Labour Prime Minister James Callaghan said: 'The goals of our education, from nursery school through to adult education, are clear enough. They are to equip children to the best of their ability for a lively, constructive, place in society, and also to fit them to do a job of work.' Nobody could disagree with this statement, but what if your students knew that there were no jobs to find, unless your family knew someone.

Quite mistakenly, in the early 1980s many school leaders in challenging urban areas, including me, saw their principal challenge as making their schools a safe haven for their students to attend, ensuring that they had enough to eat and were taught to be resistant to the external environmental pressures they constantly faced. We were unfailing in the love, concern and understanding we showed for them, but had little understanding of the benefits of raising aspirations and accepting no excuses for poor academic performance. Performance tables had not yet been introduced, and there was little sense of school accountability in terms of student progress. Leadership training and accredited qualifications were still a dream away.

On reflection, I often wonder what the effect would have been if we replaced our genuine love and care for our pupils with a form of 'tough love', coupled with 'high expectations', to help them achieve better academic outcomes, thus enhancing their social mobility. However, it was the 1980s; such phrases had yet to enter the English education lexicon and the 'glass ceiling of social mobility' was not even being talked about.

1990–2002:
The Second Headship

In 1989, I began to get itchy feet and started to look around for a new challenge. I wanted to take the leadership lessons that I had learned in my first headship and use them to become a far better leader. The headship of Parrs Wood High School in Manchester became vacant and I was lucky enough to be appointed. The school had been through a tumultuous few years and the governors were at loggerheads with the local authority, who had initiated a city-wide reorganisation of secondary education. If agreed, the reform would leave Parrs Wood without a sixth form. The previous head had successfully led the governors in fighting the city's proposals and Sir Keith Joseph, who was Secretary of State for Education at the time, stated in parliament that 'Parrs Wood is a school of proven worth' and refused the request to formally close the school's sixth form. While I wanted to lead a school with a sixth form, my first visit made me doubt Sir Keith's understanding of 'proven worth' regarding the school as a whole.

The school had opened in 1967 in prefabricated buildings with a flat roof that, unfortunately, failed to withstand the infamous rains of Manchester. By January 1990, the start of my tenure, there were buckets in most corridors and classrooms to catch the rain, the window frames had rotted and many windows were screwed shut to stop them falling out. Teachers at the school had been in prolonged industrial action and there had not been a parents' evening for four years, while school clubs, extra-curricular activities and productions were non-existent. The previous head had met regularly with the school union representatives each Monday lunchtime with, I suspect, the sole intention of antagonising them. Despite all of this, the school was still hugely popular and was achieving the best outcomes in Manchester. However, a deeper analysis of these outcomes showed that many pupils were underperforming and, in present day terminology, the school was 'coasting'. This was just the sort of challenge I was looking for. Breckfield was about working with staff who had lost self-belief, while the staff of Parrs Wood had lost motivation.

A quick analysis of the student intake showed that although the school met its admission number of 240 pupils, it was losing the children of the more aspirational parents to the highly successful independent schools in the area. Visits to the local primary schools told me of their pride in how many independent school scholarships they had achieved each year. Industrial action had prevented the staff of Parrs Wood from visiting these primary schools for over four years and there were no current primary transition programmes in place. I quickly established half-termly working lunches with the primary headteachers so that I could learn more about the 'excellent pedagogical practice' I had seen in their schools. These lunches quickly led to the development of a strong programme of primary liaison, which resulted in cross-phase subject working parties and eventually a curriculum model that brought together Year 6 and Year 7. Within two years, all of the primary pupils were regularly visiting the school and we made sure that their parents were consulted on the new 'gifted and talented' programme that we were intending to introduce. Scouse charm every time!

While the establishment of a primary liaison programme was important to stop the drift to the independent sector, so were Key Stage 4 outcomes. They were good but nowhere as good as they could be. Union action had restricted classroom visits to observe the quality of teaching but, as I carefully explained to the unions, they could not stop the headteacher from visiting lessons. I had to break down the closed classroom mentality and I used the newly introduced staff morning briefings to talk about the good practice I had seen the day before, without naming the teacher so as to avoid embarrassment. This provoked my first fierce reaction from the union representatives, as they felt I was trying to break with union guidance by encouraging them to allow more people into their classrooms to see this 'good practice'. This, apparently, was detrimental to those who were not being mentioned. When I pointed out that I was not identifying any staff, I was accused of duplicity. Would I ever?

The second part of the strategy was to raise the aspirations of both students and teachers as to what could be achieved academically. In the early 1990s, there was little use being made of data in Year 7 to predict outcomes at GCSE. I wanted staff to develop a better understanding of the talent that they had in their classrooms and encouraged a couple of newly appointed middle leaders to produce a Parrs Wood Predictor which related intake Cognitive Ability Test scores to predicted GCSE outcomes. I had to promise the unions that I would not use predictor outcomes to judge teacher performance but, for the first time, we had a tool that could identify where underperformance was happening and apply intervention strategies to improve student and teacher performance, as well as reducing in-school variation.

The third part of the strategy, intended to stop aspirational drift to the independent sector, was to ask the head of sixth form why, given that we had such a bright sixth form, nobody was ever entered for Oxford or Cambridge? His answer was somewhat surprising in that the staff considered that Oxford and Cambridge were elitist and not suitable for our students. I pushed the matter further by asking why we offered such a large range of A levels, with some subjects having less than a handful of students. He explained that we had a large range of subjects because staff enjoyed teaching A level and we did not want to lose good staff by not offering A level teaching in their subject. Having a guaranteed sixth form irrespective of Year 11 outcomes was, in my humble opinion, a barrier to raising aspirations. Once again, the status quo had to be challenged. In September 1991, I announced a minimum viability number for each sixth form subject and asked staff to determine minimum entry grades for their subject. This caused a bumpy few months but by November a new system was in place and Year 11 fully understood the grades they would need to follow their chosen subject in the sixth form. This simple measure, now universally accepted in all sixth forms, had the dual effect of sharpening Year 11 performance and producing a more academic focus in the year group. By 1995, the school was regularly appearing in lists of high-performing sixth forms in terms of A level outcomes.

However, the greatest challenge still remained. The school building was unfit for use and was way past refurbishment. The governors and I continued to challenge the local authority but positions were becoming entrenched and a fair amount of ill-feeling was developing. As I said earlier, when writing about my first headship, there were great days and challenging days. During the heat of battle with the local authority, I received the Ofsted call. We were ready for an inspection, but I had not reckoned on external interference. The chief education officer and his assistant both had children at the school. The chief officer wrote to Ofsted in his professional capacity stating that, in his opinion, my leadership was poor and that I was spending too much time stirring the governors up and insufficient time running the school. If this was not enough to contend with, the assistant chief education officer turned up, as was his right as a parent, to the then obligatory parents' evening and read out a prepared statement similar to the letter sent by his superior to Ofsted. Fortunately the inspector, under guidance from Ofsted, ignored both complaints and concentrated on inspecting the school. We managed to get a good result but I suspect that was the point in my career where I started to lose faith in local authorities.

After three years of battles and skirmishes, it was agreed that the school could try to sell a portion of its land bordering the A34 road into the city to finance the building of a new school, but one third of any money raised would be retained by the council. The campus was quite sprawling and contained some property owned by Manchester Metropolitan University who were more than eager to sell it to the school. Once purchased, this property, along with the old school building, could be demolished and the new school could be built beside where the old one stood. Working with Dave Carty of the local authority, a meeting with potential developers was organised. I was invited to speak to them about what was then a groundbreaking concept which would involve the school and a preferred bidder coming together to create a state-of-the-art school. There was a surprising amount of interest and eventually a finance organisation was chosen. The total deal was, I believe, some £20 million and the school governors were left with approximately £12.5 million to purchase the university property and build their dream school. The drawback? Once the old school was demolished the developer would build the 'Parrs Wood Entertainment Complex' and the new school would sit behind a bowling alley, a bingo hall, a cinema and several restaurants. Some two years later the new school was built and, to the best of my knowledge, the entertainment complex is still highly successful.

Success increases motivation and the school I joined in 1990 had woken up. It was now housed in new buildings and started to break new ground on many fronts. By 1998, teaching and learning coaches had been appointed and an innovative good practice group was meeting each Thursday after school. The group had established their own research arm and was nurturing many global contacts so as to improve classroom practice. There was universal staff agreement on what an outstanding lesson should look like and how we should help each other achieve that level of performance.

Alongside this academic success, the barren years of banned parents' evenings and the absence of public displays of student talent had been left well behind. The staff were producing two plays per year, as well as a staff pantomime for the students each Christmas. A great orchestra and choir were giving regular public concerts, the art department held regular community exhibitions and the physical education teachers were organising sporting awards evenings to balance the annual academic awards evening. I had learned the lessons of my first headship and 'tough love coupled with high expectations' had become our way of life but we were still not matching the independent sector in terms of Oxbridge places.

By 2002, the school was flourishing and achieving results that compared well to other leading comprehensive schools. An Ofsted inspection that year had found nothing to criticise and was very complimentary about the achievements of both staff and pupils. However, by the end of the summer term in 2004 I knew that, once again, I had taken a school as far as I could and should be looking for new challenges. During the summer break I was approached by both the National College for Teaching and Leadership (NCTL) and the Specialist Schools and Academies Trust (SSAT – now known as the Schools, Students and Teachers network). Both enquired whether I was interested in working with them to pass on the lessons I had learned during 23 years of headship. I knew that I was ready for a new challenge rather than a life of leisure and, at the age of 61, I took my first 'retirement'. I had been a headteacher for more than two decades and worked alongside school staff in producing successful academic and pastoral programmes, but the independent sector still had a stranglehold on Oxbridge places and the glass ceiling of social mobility was still there. For me, this was still the biggest failing of my leadership journey.

Lessons from my Early Headships

The Scout movement had a large influence on my development as a teenager. It encouraged character traits such as trust, loyalty, friendship, respect and courage. From an early age, I grew up with its motto of 'Be prepared'. This motto has stayed with me throughout my life and is an excellent maxim to take in to headship. Being appointed to the most senior post in a school can be both exhilarating and daunting. You can make a great start to your leadership journey by being fully prepared. Remember: 'Failure to plan is planning to fail'.

Assess the past

Every school has a backstory and it is important that you invest a great deal of time finding out as much as possible about that story before you try to change things. You need to ask yourself such questions as:

- *What does the school performance data tell you?*
- *What can you determine from the Progress 8 and Attainment 8 scores?*
- *What percentage of students gained Level 4 or Level 5 in English and mathematics?*
- *What is the school's attitude to EBacc?*
- *Is there a discernible gap in the relative performance of girls and boys? How are disadvantaged students faring?*
- *What percentage of pupils move on to further or higher education? Of those that didn't, how many became unemployed?*
- *What is the profile of the workforce?*

- *How are the finances?*
- *When was the school last inspected? What did they say about leadership? What were its strengths? What needed improving? What can Ofsted Parent View tell you?*
- *By gaining answers to questions such as these, you will start to develop an understanding of, and be prepared for, the challenges ahead of you.*

Relationship building is the bedrock of school leadership

Strong, positive relationships between headteachers and their staff can promote a conducive learning environment which, in turn, can lead to good performance outcomes from the students. These relationships are characterised by mutual respect, collaboration, trust and a common sense of purpose. It is essential that you start to build these relationships before actually taking up the post. Teachers will respect a new head that has gone to the trouble of learning names and being able to match them to faces within days of starting. This can easily be achieved by asking the office staff to prepare staff lists, organisational structures and staff photographs before you start. A few days homework, matching names to faces, will get your relationship building off to a flying start.

Values and beliefs

It is important that you have clearly thought out your beliefs and your values. Beliefs grow from life's experiences and the opinions that they form in us. For instance, you may believe, as I do, that high-quality education is a civil right. From such a belief, our values will begin to form. These values become the things we hold dear and will always defend. They will govern the way we behave, as well as how we interact and communicate with other people. Our beliefs will determine our attitudes and opinions. In your early days of headship the staff will be more interested in who you are and what you stand for than your 'grand vision' for the school.

Be continually visible

I firmly believe that new headteachers should spend as little time as possible in their office in the first few weeks of headship. As tiring as it might be, you need to be continually visible! This means being at the front gate first thing in the morning to greet your students, being on the corridors at change of lessons, being in the dining room and playgrounds during breaks and lunchtimes and being at the school gates to bid your students goodnight. It is also a good idea to tell staff that you will be dropping in to as many lessons as possible in your first few weeks; not to judge their teaching but to get a greater feel for the school's culture and climate.

Observe and listen

These are two of the most essential leadership skills and are highly important in your first few weeks of headship. Observe to see which everyday practices you think are good, which will need improving and which will need to go. Listen to as many opinions as possible without comment or debate. Your best response is 'Let me think about it'. You do not want to fight many battles before you unfurl your vision.

Build a compelling, evidence based vision

After two or three weeks, you will have had sufficient time to hone the compelling vision that you took into the job interview and can combine this with what you have seen and heard. You now need to meet with your governors, then the leadership team and, after those two meetings, the staff as a whole to talk about your observations and what you see as the way forward. Winning everyone over will need a compelling vision centered on student progress. The best schools are led, in my opinion, with every decision being based on the future success of the students. Your compelling vision must have a series of distinct and clear messages that connect the vision to the specific actions which will need to be taken. These messages must show coherence and be based on the future success of the students. Putting students first is a difficult proposition to challenge.

The burning platform

The phrase 'burning platform' was born from the Piper Alpha oil rig fire in 1988 when one of the survivors described his decision to jump off the burning oil rig as 'a reasoned decision based on inevitable death and the courage to leap in to the unknown'.

The phrase quickly became part of change management jargon to describe the urgent need for change. Simply put, it is a reality check as to what will happen if a series of proposed changes do not take place. The problem with using this approach is that there is a possibility that, if used incorrectly, it may lead to fear and confusion. Used properly, it is about gaining the level of commitment that would be needed if the change were to become successful.

Having delivered your compelling vision you need to gain the commitment of the staff to your vision. In Shakespeare's play Henry V the author attributes a speech to King Henry on St. Crispin's day just before the battle of Agincourt, where his army of some 500 soldiers were to face 3,000 well-armed French soldiers. In the speech, the King did paint the reality that the troops faced in the battle but he was also careful to describe the successes of returning home as victors and heroes. The burning platform is the battle cry for staff to have the courage and commitment to unite behind your vision.

Change is about hearts and minds not systems and procedures

If change is to be successful then the people who will carry out the change need to believe in it, understand why it is necessary and how it will help them in their everyday lives. Once they believe in the change, they will start to think differently and this will begin to alter their behaviours. If they do not believe that the change will be for the greater good, then their behaviours will soon return to those they exhibited before the change, and you will have wasted your time. You need to put as much time and energy into winning the hearts and minds of the staff as you put in to the change process itself.

Find your champions

You can lead change but, without support, you may not be able to make the change sustainable. The right 'change champions' can act as the eyes and ears of the change process, keeping their finger on the pulse and helping the process to succeed. You need to seek your champions at all levels within the school and give them the freedom to convert the resistors and blockers while driving the change forward.

Write a clear strategic plan with targets and milestones

The strategic plan is a road map of how the change is to take place. You will need to list all of the actions that need to take place, what success will look like if these actions are implemented properly, what resources will be available, what the time frame for each action will be, and who will be responsible for implementing that action.

Celebrate initial victories and small wins

Nothing succeeds like success. As the change leader, you need to be constantly searching for quick wins that show the successes that the change is bringing and publicly celebrate them. Introducing the 'feel-good' factor will give people more confidence that the change was needed and this will increase their commitment.

Look after yourself

The challenges of headship can be both invigorating and exhausting. The adrenalin that the commitment to the job creates can often disguise the drain on your energies. While you are busily managing the work–life balance of your colleagues, you must also learn to balance your own work–life balance.

Find a friend

Nobody will tell you that your leadership journey will be sunshine every day. There will be good days and challenging days. There will be uplifting days and downbeat days. There will be some days at the end of which you will be thoroughly exhausted and feel that you have achieved nothing. The worst thing you can do on days such as these is to take your problems home. Taking your stress home can sometimes strain relationships. Try to find a good friend with broad shoulders, with whom you can have the occasional coffee or even go for a drink. Your personal relationships need as much nurturing as the school.

Part 2:
Lessons from the
Charter Schools

2004–2006:
Finding a New Role in Life

January 2004 was a strange month. The everyday routine of putting on a suit, arriving early for work, giving assemblies and managing lunch queues all disappeared from my life. Most of the work for both the NCTL and the SSAT was to be spent sat alone in my home office behind my PC. I had to develop a strong sense of personal discipline, as well as a set of routines to make sure that I stayed focused. I produced detailed work schedules which provided me with what I thought was a balanced mix of work and downtime but, eventually, these soon fell away. I knew that I needed to search for new challenges.

My initial role at the NCTL was to increase the engagement of school leaders with the organisation's activities and, hopefully, generate income as a result of this increased engagement. Working with Peter Berry and his marketing team, we identified a hole in the market. The only major educational conference was run by SSAT and it was, at the time, attended mainly by secondary school leaders. Primary headteachers did not have the opportunity to attend a major conference that would look at the challenges they were facing. Within 18 months we had organised the NCTL's first national conference, attended by over 400 people, the majority of whom were from the primary sector. The main speaker at the conference was Steve Munby who was to become CEO of the college shortly afterwards. Over the years the conference has become an annual event, filling the International Convention Centre in Birmingham. Having completed this first task for the College, I was asked to transfer to the newly formed National Remodelling Team, where I toured the country with Alex Nairn, a former WHSmith executive, delivering presentations on how teacher workloads could be reduced.

Sue Williamson, at that time Deputy Director of SSAT, had asked me to work alongside Claire Mathews to help carry out a complete review of its leadership development programmes and, building upon my own experiences, bring them up to date. I wanted to take this further and embarked upon a period of worldwide research on how school leadership was being developed in different countries. The one programme that really caught my eye was an accelerated leadership programme in New York called New Leaders for New Schools (now known as New Leaders), which was identifying talented young teachers and accelerating them in to school leadership roles. However, as exciting as this sounded, it did not fit the structure of the middle and senior leadership programmes that I had been working on. Over the next six months Claire and I restructured the SSAT's entire approach to leadership development, producing a suite of programmes ranging from entry to the profession to aspirant headship.

In December 2005, having just completed the review, I received a call from Sue asking me if I had time to go to New York on her behalf to join a small team looking at a new programme that had emerged called New Leaders for New Schools. This was the very programme that caught my attention during my research and I grabbed the opportunity. Sue had been working with Steve Munby of the NCTL, Baroness Morgan of Ark Schools and Lord Adonis, Minister for Schools, in examining possible solutions to the predicted shortage of headteachers in England and they saw a New Leaders-type programme as a possible solution.

New York, January 2006

On a cold January morning in New York, our small investigative team came together to see if we could unpick the successful DNA of the New Leaders programme. Jane Creasey represented the NCTL, Nat Wei represented Ark, the multi-academy trust, and Joe Owen, a successful author and entrepreneur, completed the team. Joe and Nat had worked together as part of the initial team that had set up Teach First, under the leadership of Brett Wigdortz.

My past research was to pay dividends as I already had a fairly good knowledge of the New Leaders programme. It was founded in 2000 by Jonathan Schnur, who had worked as an education policy analyst for President Bill Clinton. The idea behind the programme was developed while Jon was attending graduate school at Harvard University. It was designed not only to accelerate talented candidates into school leadership positions, but to fundamentally change schooling in challenging urban areas. At the time of our visit the programme had become well established, with centres in New York, New Jersey, Chicago, Memphis, San Francisco and Baltimore. This unique leadership development programme had several distinct features which, in 2006, were not being used in England. Access to the programme was by nomination rather than application. Each nomination was thoroughly researched, in the belief that they had to find participants who could demonstrate a variety of strengths, such as leadership potential, high-quality communication skills and a good knowledge of the challenges facing urban schools. Each candidate was also required to demonstrate personal character traits as determination, resilience, tenacity and grit. If this was not enough, they also had to be totally aligned with the beliefs, mission and values of the programme.

The mission statement of New Leaders was to 'ensure high academic achievement for all children, especially students in poverty and students of color, by developing transformational school leaders and advancing the policies and practices that allow great leaders to succeed'. This was a unique leadership programme, in that it not only wanted to produce high-quality leaders for schools serving challenging urban areas but also sought to transform the practices and procedures of these schools in order to produce high student outcomes, where previously there had only been failure.

All nominees that fitted the desired profile were offered a place on an assessment day and, if they were successful, they would be provided with a one-year residency in a challenging urban school. Here, they would be mentored by a successful veteran principal and be trained by a variety of specialist coaches on the New Leader's staff. Following completion of the residency, each participant had to make a commitment to serve as principal or assistant principal in a challenging urban district for at least three years, during which they would still receive ongoing support from the New Leaders organisation.

Our first meeting was in the New Leaders' headquarters, where we were met by Jon Schnur and his team. It turned out to be a fascinating morning, in that we met a group of people who had completely reimagined the structure of schooling that would be necessary for successful education in very challenging urban areas and had produced a programme to find and train mission-driven people to turn failing urban schools around. The programme consisted of a summer residential training programme followed by a year's placement at leadership level in a challenging urban school, before candidates then became a principal in their own right. Throughout the placement period, and during their first two years as a principal, they would be able to continue to draw support from of a series of veteran principals who New Leaders had brought together as a coaching team.

New Leaders had a very fixed belief system. Their core ideal was that these new leaders and the teachers they would appoint to their new schools had to have an unwavering belief that every child, irrespective of their educational starting point, urban disadvantage or mother tongue, could succeed at the highest academic levels. To make this belief a reality, the training programme had to be very detailed and help the new leaders to develop the necessary skills to turn a failing school into a successful one within two years. They would have a single indicator of success and that would be the number of students who would reach the required standard for college entry before graduating from school. Most urban schools in the US had suffered from 'white flight' after legislation banned ethnicity from being an admissions factor and their population was a mixture of African American or Latino Hispanic. College entry among these young people was considered a rarity rather than the norm. New Leaders was a civil rights centred programme.

The first skill that the summer programme would focus on was each participant's ability to build a culture of high aspirations and ensure that it permeated the entire school. Developing such a culture would become an important tool in continually enthusing students to become 'college ready'. If done successfully, then teachers, parents and the students themselves would be able to understand the new methodologies used in the school and make the crucial connection between the day-to-day actions of the new approach and long-term aspirations for college entry for all of their students. If successful, gaining admittance to college would open new doors to a successful career for their students and enhance their social mobility.

Alongside this aspiration-building skill was the acquisition of the tools necessary to develop a series of social norms that would underpin the school's code of conduct. This would be strictly upheld, thus ensuring that all classroom activities were focused on the 'college-ready' ideal and were free of disruptive behaviour. The programme also laid great emphasis on developing the coaching skills of each new leader, in the firm belief that a principal successfully trained in coaching could rapidly improve teacher quality and, as we all recognise, high-quality teaching has a greater effect on student outcomes than any other school-based factor. New Leaders also believed that their leaders had to be skilled data analysts in order to quickly identify where progress was not happening and produce intervention strategies that responded to actual, rather than perceived, student need. None of these improvement strategies could be successfully deployed without the new leader also becoming fully skilled in change management and recognising that turning a school around was not an overnight operation but a step-by-step process that moved the challenging urban school from chaos to excellence. The organisation also believed that urban success could not be achieved within the present limitations to the school day. Their 'new schools' had to have a longer day in order to create more instructional time, if all students were to become 'college ready'.

It had been a long, exhausting, but exciting, morning. The New Leaders team had freely given their time and shared their research and learning while presenting a stimulating picture of school-led urban renewal. For me, the greatest challenge seemed not to be in developing a similar training programme back in England, but in finding these 'new' mission-driven leaders. New Leaders arranged for us to see the selection process in action on day two in Baltimore, where we were to observe an assessment centre in operation. We had a pre-assessment briefing arranged for 8am the next day and needed to catch an evening train from Penn Station for the two-and-a-half hour journey.

Early the next morning, we arrived at the assessment centre where the itinerary for the day was explained to us. About 12 teachers had been nominated for assessment, but careful checks on their classroom performance, set of values, communication skills and leadership potential prior to assessment had already reduced the number to six. The assessments would commence with a fish bowl debate followed by a data analysis exercise, some role play and an in-depth interview. Each exercise was to be timed to the minute and it was intended to be a deliberately gruelling day for each nominee. This seemed a far cry from a tour of the school, presentation, demonstration lesson and formal interview that was the present process back home.

The assessments commenced with all six nominees seated around a table. After everyone had introduced themselves, they were invited to open the envelopes in front of them to reveal the purpose of the 'fish bowl' debate. It was to be based on a challenging question which would require some thought.

'The No Child Left Behind Act was introduced in 2002. Why, some four years later, are children still being left behind?'

The participants were then given five minutes to prepare their arguments before the exercise formally began. We sat alongside the observers at the side of the room who shared their success criteria with us. Their judgements were to be based on five criteria: to assess how each participant interacted with their peers in a high-pressure situation; to identify participants who could lead without dominating a discussion; to assess how actively each participant listened to the views of others and take on their thoughts; to assess the depth of their critical thinking and, finally, how participants created openings to draw others into the debate. I had not seen such an exercise before but within minutes I was able to detect who the skilled communicators and best critical thinkers were.

The data analysis exercise lasted 45 minutes. Each participant was given a spreadsheet outlining the performance of students in an urban elementary school. They had to assess the performance of the school as a whole, identify specific weaknesses and suggest both short- and long-term improvement strategies. Given the amount of data they were provided with, 45 minutes was not a long time, but the exercise was intended to be difficult and designed to identify those participants who could think analytically, creatively, strategically and quickly.

The role play was incredibly challenging. Participants were put into a room with an observer and a professional actor who told them he would be playing three roles. The first was a child who had been sent out of class and was reluctant to discuss the reasons behind the teacher's actions. As he went into character, each participant had to draw deeply upon their empathic skills and try to get the child to open up and discuss why he had been sent to the principal. After seven minutes, irrespective of where the participant was up to, the actor suddenly closed the scenario down and announced that he was leaving the room and, when he returned, he would be role playing the father of the child. After 15 seconds, the door flew open and in he came yelling and screaming about the racist behaviour of the teacher, citing various incidents that his family had 'endured' over the years. Once again, the participant had seven minutes to calm the parent down and reassure him that the incident would be dealt with. After exactly seven minutes the actor changed roles once again and became the teacher who had been accused of 'picking on the child'. During this final role play it quickly became obvious that the teacher had a problem with the ethnicity of the family. At the end of the three scenarios, I caught up with the observer and asked her what she had been looking for. Communication skills, empathy, the ability to diffuse difficult situations and, above all, how the participant dealt with the teacher's behaviour. I suggested that these participants were still at the application stage and had very little previous experience of dealing with such challenging situations. She agreed but stressed that it was potential she was looking for rather than a polished performance.

At the end of a long afternoon each participant had a 45-minute interview that assessed their values and beliefs. There were many 'what if' questions but the underlying rationale behind the grilling was to test each participant's belief that all children could succeed, irrespective of their educational starting point, urban disadvantage or mother tongue, if given appropriate support.

Finally, the participants were thanked and sent home while the observers became involved in what was termed a 'wash up', where a final decision was made as to who would be accepted onto the programme.

It was fairly obvious that, in 2006, we had nothing this rigorous back home. It had been a long, hard day with lots to think about and debate but we needed to head back to New York where, on day three, we were to observe the coaching programme in action.

We arrived at the charter school at 8am the next morning to meet the newly appointed principal and his veteran coach. They explained that, during the day, we would observe a 'support and challenge' meeting that the coach would hold with the principal, tour the school with both of them to verify the improvements that had taken place since the coaches last visit, watch the coach quality assure the principal's training of a young teacher and then check on the overall quality of the teaching across the school, before a final 'wash up' meeting at the end of the day. It was to be another strenuous day but it could just provide evidence that the programme was being successful.

The 'support and challenge' meeting was very data orientated, with the coach grilling the new leader on the latest set of school data. The discussion included a forensic examination of data ranging from attendance and punctuality, to student progress, to teacher quality and how identified training needs were being met. At the end of the discussion an action plan, which the principal agreed to implement, was drawn up.

How I wished I had such support in 1980!

During the interview, the principal had outlined the improvements that had taken place since the coach's last visit. The next 45 minutes were spent touring the school so as to ensure that these improvements were in place and checking that the next steps were included in the improvement plan.

Quality assuring the principal's coaching ability was another first for me. We entered a classroom with the principal and the coach, who sat at either side of the room in the back row. The coach took a small pair of headphones out of his briefcase and put them on his head while the principal took out a very small microphone and switched it on. Quickly glancing at the teacher, I realised that the small device in her ear was not a hearing aid but a miniature speaker that could pick up the principal's comments as he quietly coached her classroom performance. I was used to the age-old practice of observation followed by a reflective discussion but this was active coaching in action. After the session, the teacher joined the principal and coach to discuss how effective the help had been. Once again, a steep learning curve in how to improve classroom practice.

Deciding on the overall quality of teaching across the school caused me a few problems in that I did not see any group work and found little evidence of differentiation of task to match perceived ability. It was as if I had slipped back in time to very traditional didactic teaching. We had become a nation of progressives and here I was watching very traditional teaching producing amazing gains in outcomes. More food for thought for our journey back home.

On reporting our findings back to the DfE a decision was made to try to emulate the success of New Leaders and produce a fast track leadership programme for selecting and training new leaders for challenging urban schools in London. Working with Nat Wei and Jay Altman, an inspiring American educator, who were both then working for Ark Schools, we co-founded what we would later call 'Future Leaders' with funding from the DfE, the NCTL and Ark. I was asked to become director of training and charged with writing the training programme and finding four 'veteran' coaches.

If we were to create a transformational leadership programme for challenging urban schools then we had to know where the real challenges lay. By 2006, the DfE were able, for the first time, to examine the national gaps in attainment between disadvantaged students and their more advantaged counterparts. The 2006 GCSE cohort were the first year group for whom it was possible to identify not only students receiving free school meals when they were in Year 11 and taking their GCSEs but, also, whether they received free school meals at any stage of their secondary school career. The analysis showed that the proportion of free school meal students achieving five or more 'A*–C' grade GCSEs and equivalents in 2005 was just over 30%, while the proportion of students not receiving free school meals was almost 60%. Our challenge would be to produce a leadership programme aimed at equipping participants with the skills to transform these outcomes and close this attainment gap.

After consulting many young teachers, we decided that the programme should be called 'Future Leaders'. It would have the distinct mission of addressing educational inequality through the development of the next generation of leaders for challenging urban schools, so that more schools in disadvantaged areas could offer their students a better future and enhanced social mobility.

By the end of May the training programme had been written, 20 participants had been identified, four former headteachers had been appointed as coaches and our first summer school was already planned. After the summer training, each participant was to take up a residency position on the leadership team of a school serving a challenging urban area. However, as a team we were convinced that training and coaching was not going to be enough to align the hearts and minds of our participants with our mission. We had to find the funding to finance a study tour of successful charter schools in the US to allow the participants in Future Leaders to see at first hand the performance gains that leaders with 'can-do' attitudes could bring about.

I was no longer in a position to lead a school in breaking the glass ceiling and enhancing the social mobility of young people in challenging urban areas but, now, I had the chance to be part of a mission-driven organisation that had the ceiling firmly in its sights.

Reflections on the visit to New Leaders

The National Professional Qualification for Headship (NPQH) was introduced in 1997. It was intended to prepare experienced teachers for headship through training in leadership and management techniques, with the eventual aim of improving school standards. The programme provided some tutorial support and was delivered by experienced headteachers. I was a programme tutor from 1998 until 2003. It was a good programme but, in retrospect, it lacked the mission-driven approach of the New Leaders' programme.

Vision and mission
In 2006 vision and mission statements were not in common usage in English schools. At the time of writing most school websites carry a vision or mission statement but, unfortunately, there still exists confusion regarding the difference between vision and mission. Mission statements should define a schools purpose and primary objectives. They should be written in the present tense and explain to the outside world why the school exists. Vision statements also define a school's purpose but they focus on the long-term goals and aspirations it wishes to achieve. They are designed to be uplifting, inspiring and timeless.

To try to further define the difference between vision and mission, let's look at the Coca-Cola organisation.

Coca-Cola
Our Roadmap starts with our mission, which is enduring. It declares our purpose as a company and serves as the standard against which we weigh our actions and decisions.

- *To refresh the world...*
- *To inspire moments of optimism and happiness...*
- *To create value and make a difference.*

Our vision serves as the framework for our Roadmap and guides every aspect of our business by describing what we need to accomplish in order to continue achieving sustainable, quality growth.

- **People:** *Be a great place to work where people are inspired to be the best they can be.*
- **Portfolio:** *Bring to the world a portfolio of quality beverage brands that anticipate and satisfy people's desires and needs.*
- **Partners:** *Nurture a winning network of customers and suppliers, together we create mutual, enduring value.*
- **Planet:** *Be a responsible citizen that makes a difference by helping build and support sustainable communities.*
- **Profit:** *Maximize long-term return to shareowners while being mindful of our overall responsibilities.*
- **Productivity:** *Be a highly effective, lean and fast-moving organization.*

The company's mission is to 'refresh the world and bring happiness' through the consumption of its products, while its vision is how they intend to bring this about through their now famous '6 Ps' of people, portfolio, partners, planet, profit and productivity. Each of these seven can be measured to see how much progress is being made to achieve the mission.

(www.coca-cola.ca/our-company/mission-vision-values)

The New Leaders' organisation has the following powerful mission statement:

> 'We **prepare education leaders to deliver breakthrough results** in *America's highest-need schools and advocate for* **policies that enable great leaders – and their students – to thrive.***'

Their vision is to build and maintain an organisation that will:

- *ensure high academic achievement for students in poverty and students of colour by training school leaders to drive improvement in schools with low test scores and high poverty rates*
- *ensure that these leaders are fully supported by a high-quality coaching and support programme*
- *advance policies and practices that allow these leaders to reach their goals and their students to thrive.*

The mission is the start of their road map and their vision is the framework that guides all of their actions.

Skills for headship

New Leaders has a clear understanding of the skills that they need to develop in their new leaders if they are to achieve their mission of achieving breakthrough results for their students. Among these skills are:

- *excellent communication skills*
- *deep, pedagogical knowledge*
- *the ability to develop a culture of high expectations throughout their school*
- *how to analyse data forensically so as to determine where support and intervention is necessary*
- *how to induct new teachers into the school ethos*
- *how to coach these teachers so that they can achieve outstanding results*
- *how to deliver effective feedback*
- *how to build strong teams capable of enacting ambitious school improvement plans*
- *when, and how, to hold a challenging conversation about individual performance.*

For me, the greatest challenge any principal can rise to is the breaking of the glass ceiling that prevents upward social mobility for too many of our students. Becoming proficient in these skills could help you rise to that challenge.

2007:
Leading my First Study Tour

I had not been able to accompany the first study tour to the US for Future Leaders' participants and their residency headteachers in October 2006, as I had a long-standing contractual agreement with, what was then, the Teacher Training Agency that I was morally obliged to keep. However, the feedback on the visit was diametrically split. The Future Leaders' participants had been well briefed on what to expect as they saw the rhetoric of their training in daily practice. On the other hand, we had not given the headteachers of the residency schools enough of an explanation of the practice they were about to observe and their reaction was similar to my own when I had visited my first charter school. Phrases such as 'locked in the dark ages' and 'have they never heard of child-centred education' were thrown at the Future Leaders' coaches. It was an early sign of the progressive or traditional debate that still rages on Twitter today. Unfortunately, both sides claimed to be educational Jedi and, to this day, still see their opponents as the educational equivalent of Sith.

Although there are many different descriptions of a traditionalist approach to education, I think it can be summed up by three inter-related components. For me, these are the following:

1. Education is about the passing on of content knowledge and skills that students are expected to learn and master.

2. This learning cannot be mastered unless there are rules and behaviour norms that form habits of conformity within the school's code of conduct,

3. There has to be systems of organisation which govern the daily life of the

school, such as the length of the school day, fixed lesson times, formal examinations, etc.

On the other side of the argument, progressive education is based on the belief that students learn best in real-life activities which are meaningful to them. A progressive teacher will provide not just learning opportunities but also real-world experiences and activities that relate to the actual lives of the students. A typical progressivist slogan is 'learn by doing'. They believe that learning should be child centred, with the curriculum and teaching methods being developmentally appropriate and responsive to each individual child's strengths and interests.

In 2014, Professor Robert Coe, of Durham University, co-authored a Sutton Trust report on what makes good teaching. Coe is honest in that he readily identifies that defining effective teaching is not easy. For the purpose of the report he defined effective teaching as: 'Teaching which leads to improved student outcomes in achievement using outcomes that matter to future success.' Taking this to its logical conclusion, if any type of teaching is to be effective it must be judged by the resulting outcomes of its students. It would have been really useful to have this report to hand as I led the second wave of Future Leaders and their residency heads on the second study tour of New York in October 2007, but it was seven years too early.

I was determined to avoid the traditionalist versus progressive debate and decided that we would give the residency heads a better briefing before they visited their first charter school. At 7am on a damp and dark Wednesday morning in October, I found myself using the coach driver's microphone to give a 20-minute talk to a group of very sleepy people about the school that we were going to visit. I explained the socio-economics of the neighbourhood, the traditional pedagogical practice that we would see and the need to look beyond that, as we headed towards North Star Academy, a 5–11 elementary school, in Newark, New Jersey.

I explained that research had shown me that Newark was one of the poorest cities in the country, with almost half of its children living below the poverty line. New Jersey statistics showed that, at the time, Newark children we_e less healthy, less likely to finish high school, and less likely to reach adulthood than other children around the state.

I added in some facts about the intake of the academy; students entering North Star are often significantly behind their state peers, with their test scores often being below the Newark district average, which was one of the lowest performing districts in the state. Admission to the school was by random lottery. This resulted in nearly all North Star students being of African-American or Latino-Hispanic heritage, with 80% qualifying for free or reduced price lunch and, in terms of role models and aspiration, 90% of their parents never having the opportunity to graduate from college.

I told them that North Star had been co-founded by Norman Atkins and Jamie Verilli in 1997. Norman Atkins had spent five years in New York co-leading the Robin Hood Foundation, whose principal aim was to break the cycle of poverty that limited people's aspirations and life chances. He realised that the answer had to lie in early years education but he had no experience of how to set up a school designed to develop the aspirations of disadvantaged children. It was by chance that he was given the telephone number of James Verilli. Jamie had been a teacher and principal of a small 'low fee' private school in Newark that was trying to give a good education to poor, low-income families. They agreed to meet up in a local restaurant and spent some four hours exploring each other's views on what a great school should be doing. This led to the founding of North Star Academy, the first school on our study tour. The name 'North Star' had been chosen after consultation with parents, as it had long been the symbol of hope and freedom within the black community. Frederick Douglass had used this symbol in the struggle against slavery by naming his nineteenth century abolitionist newspaper *The North Star,* as it was this star that guided escaping slaves from the southern states towards emancipation in the northern states. Every facet of North Star's culture would support the vision of 'seeing the star', guiding students along a path to success in college and in life.

I explained to the tour group that the founders' mission statement was to serve Newark children by building a school where students would participate in a rigorous, ten-month long annual academic program with longer school days that would give them the means to become 'college ready' and that this would be underpinned by a set of values that centred on caring, courage, justice, respect and responsibility.

I had previously asked the Future Leaders' participants to keep a reflective learning journal throughout the visit, based on these three questions.

1. Identify the practices that strike you as being different from your school practices back in England.

2. Why are these practices in place and how effective are they in raising student outcomes?

3. What, as a result of the visit, would you do differently in your residency schools when you return to England?

Shortly before arriving at the academy we agreed that, before making any judgements, our principal line of enquiry would be the overall school ethos, how close this ethos was to the founder's mission statement, how behaviour was being managed and the quality of the outcomes that the teaching was producing. Coming to this agreement prior to walking through the front door of the school helped me alleviate a progressive – traditionalist debate among the residency headteachers when we came to summarise the visit.

We arrived at the school just before 8am. Our first sight was of a teacher standing at the school gate shaking hands with each student as they arrived. 'That's nice, but why?' enquired one of the residency heads. Before I could reply, his Future Leader jumped in to explain that teacher–student emotional engagement through a formal greeting and smile set the tone for the day – well done the summer training team! We went into the school hall where the early risers were queuing for a breakfast of yoghurt, cereal or cereal bar and an orange drink. Having collected their breakfast they went and sat with their class group and teacher, who ensured a 'silent' breakfast, while she checked last night's homework. The school principal waved us over to one side of the hall where we were treated to coffee and cookies – apparently a charter teacher's favourite breakfast. Having greeted us, he outlined our day. Once the school day had started for the youngsters, he had set aside half an hour to talk to us about the school and then we were free to roam, as there was an open door policy to all classrooms for visitors but we were not to interrupt the learning process by chatting to the students. He wanted them on task at all times. However, he would break this rule and allow us to join a breakfast table where we could talk to them in – he said laughingly – hushed tones before their day began.

When breakfast had ended school notices were given out accompanied by praise 'shout outs' for students who had worked hard the previous day and demonstrated the school values. This was followed by the whole student body pledging allegiance to the flag and then each table following their teacher, in silent straight lines, to their classroom. Glancing around the hall we noticed a total absence of litter. The principal explained that, if litter had been found then the whole class would have to return in silence and that would hurt their teacher and nobody wanted that. Strong emotional teacher–student relationships were the key to good behaviour.

We were then taken to an empty classroom where the principal outlined the school's mission and ethos, as well as its 'high expectations and no excuses' culture. He said that he hoped we would see both academic rigour and a joyful student culture in each classroom, adding that we would need to look carefully for the culture as many visitors couldn't see the joy of learning and succeeding through the silence of total focus and engagement. He went on to explain the school maxim – 'every minute counts' – meant a minute wasted was a minute worth of learning lost. Everything we would see was intentional, ranging from the motivational signage in the hallways, to the silent line-ups outside of classrooms, the shaking of hands on entry, to the well-planned seating arrangements, and right through to the challenging questions the teachers would ask to check students' understanding and progress. He stressed that time was the enemy in making his students 'college ready', which is why the school operated a ten month year and a longer school day than other Newark public schools. Asked about educational starting points on entry, he replied 'We meet them where they are educationally and, to ensure they receive the best education possible, we make our teachers better faster through regular feedback and personalised professional development.' As we were winding up, a Future Leader asked him how his teachers achieved silent walking in straight lines with such young children. He laughed and said we have our hallway rhyme which he proceeded to chant and mime

'Hands by your sides

All eyes forward

Legs walking safely

Lips zipped – and throw the key out of the window'

'Model it, practise it and don't let your standards slip – high expectations and no excuses,' he said, with a big smile. 'Enjoy your day.'

We quickly split up into small groups and started to visit classrooms. The first thing we noticed was that class numbers were smaller than we expected, with about 24 pupils in each class. This gave each teacher more time with individual students. There was great emphasis on oral communication, with teachers only accepting whole-sentence answers. The response to 'What is six times nine?' had to be in the acceptable form of 'Six times nine is 54, Miss'. This was deliberate practice not only to stop monosyllabic answers but to increase the confidence of each child in public speaking. You could sense the actual excitement in each classroom but never did we see it distract anyone from their learning. The behaviour instructions were silent, conveyed by hand or facial signal and quickly followed by the students. Emotional engagement between the teachers and their classes was very strong, behavioural engagement was spot on and the combination of these two factors was obviously producing high levels of cognitive engagement. There were constant teacher exhortations that each student could change history by becoming college ready and following their dream. Asked regularly what their dream was, there was an automatic and excited response 'To go to college and follow my dream'. When you hear six- and seven-year-old children repeating this mantra you quickly realise that it is not cloning but the continual raising of aspirations from a very early age. The teaching was quite didactic in that we did not see any group work or differentiation of task. Each teacher pitched their expectations high and scaffolded down to meet individual student need. Despite the residency headteachers' doubts about the school's pedagogical approach, an examination of the academy's progress scores showed that they were outperforming their more affluent, suburban district peers on New Jersey state assessments. They were making great strides in closing the achievement gap, opening up the glass ceiling to college and enhancing their students' social mobility.

At the end of our visit the coach journey back to the hotel was quite subdued. I asked the Future Leaders' participants to write up a few learning points before they went out to eat. Turning to one of the more experienced residency heads, I asked her what she had thought of the day. Looking pensive, she replied 'I can be critical of their teaching methods but not the progress and outcomes these methods are producing – I have a lot to think about.' These teachers were preparing their students to break the glass ceiling to college entry from a very early age and that was a big message to take home.

Our second day was to be spent visiting Amistad Academy in New Haven, which meant a 6.30am start from our hotel. Still very sleepy, and clutching large, paper cups of coffee, the Future Leaders and their residency heads boarded the coach. It was obvious that some of them had enjoyed their second night in New York and, as it was going to be at least a 90-minute drive, I decided to let everyone sleep until we were nearer the school before giving them an outline of what we were expecting to see.

We were to be met by Dacia Toll, a former teacher and Rhodes Scholar, who had worked for 18 months planning the school before becoming its first principal, and Mathew Taylor, the current principal. The school was named after the schooner La Amistad, which became a symbol in the abolition movement after 53 West African captives on the ship staged a rebellion in 1839. Once again, an inspirational name for an ambitious project. A replica of the ship is based in the New Haven harbour.

The academy had opened in 1999 to serve New Haven middle school students in grades 5–8 (10–14-year-olds). The initial intake of 84 fifth and sixth-graders subsequently expanded to 270 students. After five years the academy was receiving eight applications for each available place. Admission was by lottery and, as Dacia admitted to us later that morning, she didn't like telling parents that getting a good education was based on luck in the lottery. However, it also meant that the academy couldn't select by ability and had to adjust its instructional programmes each year to the starting levels of the intake. It became clear by 2003 that more admissions would be needed if demand was to be met. This led to the establishment of Achievement First which, with Dacia as CEO, would start to open new schools based on the Amistad model.

In 2007, Amistad was a kindergarten to Grade 9 academy with a student population consisting of around 60% African-American children alongside 30% of Hispanic origin. All Achievement First schools have the same mission statement:

> 'The mission of Achievement First is to deliver on the promise of equal educational opportunity for all of America's children. We believe that all children, regardless of race or economic status, can succeed if they have access to a great education. Achievement First schools provide all of our students with the academic and character skills they need to graduate from top colleges, to succeed in a competitive world and to serve as the next generation of leaders in our communities.'

Once again, a mission-driven belief that all children can succeed given access to a great education but, for the first time, the phrase 'character skills' is used. An admission that breaking the glass ceiling into college would require not only great teaching but strategies to enhance such character traits as determination, resilience and perseverance if their students were to succeed. This mission statement was underpinned by a set of values known as REACH to guide the students' journey. REACH stood for respect, enthusiasm, achievement, citizenship and hard work. Put simply, the mission of every Achievement First academy was to achieve dramatic gains in both academic performance and character development so that as many students as possible could graduate and enter college.

From Monday to Thursday students were expected to attend from 7:30am to 3.30pm, resulting in a school day that is an hour and a half longer than that of New Haven public schools. On Fridays, students start at 7:30am but are dismissed at 1pm, giving teachers time to plan together and engage in professional development. During the nine-and-a-half-hour school day, students spend three-and-a-half-hours on reading and writing and, after school, all students have homework assignments that include independent reading.

As we neared the academy, and having delivered my 'background briefing', we agreed that this time our line of enquiry would be to look for evidence that, irrespective of teaching style, whether dramatic academic gains were being made, whether character development was evident and if the teaching methodology resulted in more students breaking the glass ceiling and entering college each year.

The first thing we saw on entering the academy was a large poster headed 'Commitment to Excellence', that read:

> *'I have the power to create a great life for myself. I have high standards and always behave in a way that brings me closer to my goals of success in high school, college, and life. I follow the rules to keep my community safe and strong. To achieve my goals, I will follow the REACH values.'*

Passing by this poster, we saw the REACH messages. Respect was explained by the following words:

> *'Treat teachers Like PLATINUM: My teachers care about me and my family. I never talk back, roll my eyes, or suck my teeth. My teachers are here to help me be my best, so I treat them with TOTAL RESPECT.'*

The enthusiasm poster read:

> *'Bring an A+ attitude into school each day – I'm excited to climb the mountain to college. I always bring a positive attitude. I never whine, pout, or act out when things don't go my way.'*

These messages were deliberately designed to modify behaviours and increase aspiration. The school may have laminated them for display but they expected them to be carried out each day by their students.

Having met our hosts and listened to their outline of the mission, vision, ethos and values that permeated the school, Mathew Taylor asked us to look out for two specific words during our visit – 'rigour' and 'relentless'. He explained that these were the two words that the academy encouraged all staff, parents and community members to use when explaining the Achievement First approach. He hoped we would see that expectations were clearly communicated both verbally and visually to the students. He further explained that, just as we had seen in North Star, each classroom had an open door policy, but asked if would try not to disturb any student who was 'on-task'. To our surprise, he said that he had arranged for us to meet a group of parents later in the day so that we could see how the school–parent partnership was forged.

Moving down the clean, bright hallways towards the classroom we saw that the walls were decorated with examples of high-quality, inspirational student art, as well as portraits of successful Latino and African-American role models. On the door of each classroom was a pennant signalling the college that the teacher had attended. Aspiration was clearly being signposted. Inside every classroom a smaller version of the 'Commitment to Excellence' poster that we had seen in the main entrance was clearly displayed. The raising of aspirations was high on the academy's agenda.

Each homeroom classroom had the week and that day's attendance clearly displayed. Good attendance was a prominent feature of the academy. 'If they are not here they cannot learn' we were told. Each morning, right at the start of school, attendance was recorded and, if a parent has not already contacted the academy the home would be telephoned or visited. In signing the home–school agreement each parent commits to not only contacting the academy before 7.30am if their child is not going to attend that day, but also agrees that their child will attend the summer 'catch-up' academy if their attendance falls below the minimum target level. Parents also agree not to book holidays during term time. The fact that the academy has eight applications for each place demonstrates the willingness to comply with these tight rules.

We spent some time looking at the curriculum model that the teachers were employing. It was very well planned in terms of content, goals, objectives, sequencing and assessment. The academy had obviously worked backwards from their long-term goal of making all students 'college ready' and defined the standards that all students were expected to master at each grade level so that success in their present grade became the foundation for the following year. Such an approach made learning seamless as the students grew older. To ease workload, Achievement First had brought in expertise to write high-quality lessons. The academy's academic dean then worked with the teachers to ensure that they completely understood the content and were able to plan the delivery of the lessons so that it was appropriate to the context of their class. It was a highly structured and challenging approach. Each lesson plan pitched the objectives high and scaffolded down so that all students reached the given objective. Differentiation was not in content but in the level of support and time given to individual students so that everyone achieved mastery.

Another feature was 'real time assessment'. Every six weeks, all students took a series of short tests that were intended to measure whether they were actually mastering what they had been taught. The assessment results of each student would be reviewed by the academic dean, who then identified students who were going to need additional specific support and worked with the teachers in planning this support. When pushed, the dean readily admitted that the tests also helped him to identify which teachers needed additional coaching, if standards were to be kept high.

Student behaviour throughout the long school day was incredibly good. Routines were quickly followed and it was difficult to find any one student 'off task'. We constantly heard teacher exhortations for students to be rigorous in their work and students responding with classroom chants, such as 'Capital letters start a sentence – full stops bring it to a close', followed by two handclaps. Rigour and fun!

Further investigation revealed that there was a merit and demerit system for upholding the REACH values. Each week the academy published a printout of the total merits earned in the form of a paycheck; this was converted into 'scholar dollars' which could be spent at the student store or used to buy special privileges or places on a field trip.

Later in the afternoon we met the group of parents who had been invited to join us. They were very enthusiastic about the academy and appreciative of how it involved them in their child's education. They told us that all new parents were visited after being successful in the lottery and were taken through the academy's philosophy of high expectations and what was required from each parent if they wanted their child to become 'college ready'. All of this was contained in the home–school agreement that parents were expected to sign before formal admission took place. This contract had three sections. In the first section, the academy outlined their commitments to each child and their family. In the second section, parents had to commit to high levels of attendance for their child, a quiet place to do homework and 20 minutes independent reading each night, including weekends. In the final section, each student had to commit themselves to upholding the REACH values and keeping up with the overall expectations of the academy.

An example of a home school agreement is shown below:

AMISTAD ACADEMY
School-Student-Parent Contract

Amistad Academy commits to a partnership between parents, students, and school staff to provide the best possible education for our students. In order to achieve our very ambitious goals, we must work together.

Teacher's Commitment

1. *High Quality Education* – We commit to providing a high-quality education and to going the extra mile for our students. We will work longer school hours, teach during the summer, and always offer our students the best we have.
2. *Support and Respect* – We will appreciate, support, and respect every student.
3. *Communication* – We will communicate regularly with parents about their child's progress and make ourselves available in person and by phone. We will return parent phone calls within 24 hours.
4. *Homework* – We will assign productive, worthwhile homework every night to reinforce and support skills and concepts learned in class.
5. *Fairness* – We will enforce Amistad's REACH values consistently and fairly. When students are disciplined or suspended, or when students deserve recognition for their accomplishments, we will inform their parents promptly.
6. *Safety* – We will always protect the safety, interests, and rights of all individuals.

Signed: _____ Date: _____

Parent's / Guardian's Commitment

1. *Timeliness/Attendance* – I understand that every school day is important and that it is my responsibility to get my child to school every day on time (7:30 A.M.). If my child needs to miss school, I will contact the school. I will also make sure my child attends Summer Academy, and I will never schedule family vacations during school time.
2. *Support & Homework* – I will always help my child in the best way I know how, and I will do whatever it takes for my child to learn. I will provide a quiet space for my child to study and, if necessary, I will check my child's homework every night. If my child struggles with homework and is required to attend after-school Homework Club, I will arrange for transportation home at 6:00 p.m.
3. *Independent Reading* – I will insist that my child reads for at least 20 minutes a night (including all three days of the weekend), and I will never sign the reading log unless I have personally seen my child read.
4. *Communication* – I will make myself available to my child and all of his/her teachers. I will return phone calls from school staff within 24 hours. If I am asked to attend a meeting regarding my child's education or behavior, I will be there.
5. *Uniform* – I will send my child to school every day in the Amistad uniform.
6. *REACH and School Rules* – I will make sure that my child learns to live up to Amistad's REACH values and high standards of behavior. I, not the school, am responsible for the behavior and actions of my child. I know that my child may lose privileges or have other disciplinary consequences if he/she violates the REACH values.
7. *Attendance at Parent Meetings*: I will attend all required parent meetings, including Back-to-School Night, two Report Card Nights, and "Biggest Job" seminars during the year. I will also complete all the homework I am assigned.

Signed: _____ Date: _____

Student's Commitment

1. *My Best Effort* – I understand that my education is important, and I will always work, think, and behave in the best way I know how and do whatever it takes for my fellow students and me to learn.
2. *Attendance and Timeliness* – I will come to school every day on time (by 7:30 A.M.) and stay until 5:00 P.M. (or later if I have Homework Club or other responsibilities). If I need to miss class, I will ask for and make up all missed assignments.
3. *Uniform* – I will wear my Amistad uniform properly every day and follow the school dress code.
4. *Homework* – I will complete all of my homework and reading every night. I will not offer excuses; I will seek the help I need to complete all my homework in a top-quality manner.
5. *Communication* – I will raise my hand to ask for help if I do not understand something. I will make myself available to my teachers and parents about any concerns they might have.
6. *Responsibility* – If I make a mistake, I will tell the truth and accept responsibility for my actions
7. *REACH* – I understand the REACH values, and I will live up to them every day. I will follow all school rules so as to protect the safety, interests, and rights of all individuals. I understand that I may lose privileges and have other disciplinary consequences if I break rules or do not live up to the REACH values.

Signed: _____ Date: _____

Sitting quietly on the long journey back to our hotel, we reflected on the lines of enquiry that we had set ourselves before visiting the school.

Prior to entering the school we had agreed that our lines of enquiry would be to look for evidence that, irrespective of teaching style, dramatic academic gains were being made, whether character development was evident and if the teaching methodology resulted in more students breaking the glass ceiling and entering college each year. We had not only seen a plethora of evidence to satisfy each of these lines of enquiry, but that Amistad was really trying to smash the glass ceiling that their students faced in gaining entry to college.

The third and final day of the study tour needed only a 30-minute drive. At 6.45am, we were on the coach heading for KIPP in the Bronx, which had a great reputation and had been started up by Dave Levin. KIPP is an acronym for the 'Knowledge is Power Programme'. It had been founded by Mike Feinberg and Dave Levin who had both joined 'Teach for America' in 1992. 'Teach for America' had been started by Wendy Kopp in 1989 in response to the dual challenges of continuous poor outcomes of low income youngsters in urban and rural schools and a national teacher shortage. Public schools, decades after desegregation, seemed unable to make up for the long-term effects of lack of aspiration, poverty and many other deeply rooted social injustices that faced the youngsters in their schools. Wendy's plan was to recruit an army of high-performing college graduates who, after a brief period of training, would teach in the most challenging schools that were facing the real effects of the teacher shortage.

Levin and Feinberg both were assigned in Houston where they were initially overwhelmed by the difficulty of imparting knowledge to raucous and unruly inner-city students. Refusing to give up, Levin asked Harriet Ball, a very good and experienced teacher who was working alongside him at Bastian Elementary School, to mentor and coach himself and Mike Feinberg. From Harriet, they learned the importance of good classroom management if students were to make progress. Watching Harriet teach, they realised how effective she was in keeping the classroom vibrant, enjoyable and full of energy. She had a 'high expectations and no excuses' approach with all of her students. One of her principle strategies was the use of mnemonic chants to firmly attach good study habits, as well as the essential rules of grammar and mathematics to eager young minds. One of her most famous chants was:

> 'You gotta read, baby, read
> You gotta read, baby, read
> The more you read the more you know
> 'Cause knowledge is power
> Power is money, and
> I want it!'

According to Levin and Feinberg this chant led to a thirst for reading among her students, which resulted in incredible improvements in reading ages.

'Knowledge is power' became the name of the revolutionary new approach they were to forge in their urban classrooms.

After meeting Rafe Esquith, an award-winning instructor in Los Angeles, they discovered the merits of a longer school day to allow more teaching to take place, as well as the need for a content-rich knowledge based curriculum if they were to help low-income and ethnic minority students in gaining the high academic standards they would need if they were to go to college.

They added to these strategies a 'broken windows' discipline approach that is well recognised by successful school leaders. They believed that any misbehaviour left unaddressed would increase the likelihood of repetition and distract students from their learning, hence the mantra – 'Work hard. Be nice'. This rigid approach to discipline led some cynics to rename the programme 'Kids In Prison', but this cynicism is soon destroyed when you see the outcomes it produces.

KIPP's 2007 'Annual Report Card' is a good way to get a better understanding of the strengths of the Knowledge is Power Programme at that time. The report examines the performance of every KIPP school that had been open for more than a year. Statistics contained in the report showed that:

- 43 out of KIPP's 49 featured schools met the programme's annual yearly progress goals.
- National tests showed a near-doubling of scores by students completing fifth through eighth grades in KIPP schools.
- 67% of KIPP fifth-grade classes outperformed their local districts on state reading and English exams and 63% on mathematics exams. Every eighth-grade class outperformed its local districts in both reading and mathematics.
- On Algebra tests, 93% of KIPP classes outperformed local district classes.

Admission to KIPP schools is also by lottery, thus ruling out selection by ability, ethnicity or zip code. However, in most KIPP schools more than 95% of their students are of African-American or Latino-Hispanic origin and over 85% are eligible for free or subsidised meals. KIPP was clearly having a huge effect on the progress of these 'Kippsters'. Generally their students are well below average on entry compared to the state-wide averages almost everywhere, but above state average when graduating.

A fundamental part of the KIPP approach is parental involvement and alignment. After a student is selected from the lottery, KIPP asks each family and the student to confirm that they still wanted to accept the offer of a place at KIPP. To make sure that they understand the ethos and high expectations that are required, a home visit is arranged during the summer vacation by a member of the school staff to discuss these expectations. At the end of each home visit the student, their parent(s) and the visiting teacher all sign a KIPP 'commitment to excellence' agreement to fulfil specific responsibilities, promising that they will do everything in their power to help the student succeed and work hard in order to gain entry to college. A sample of the commitment agreement is published below.

All of their methodology is brought together under five operational principles or 'pillars' which, quoting from their literature are:

High Expectations
KIPP schools have clearly defined and measurable high expectations for academic achievement and conduct. Students, parents, teachers, and staff create and reinforce a culture of achievement and support through a range of formal and informal rewards and consequences for academic performance and behaviour.

Choice and Commitment
Students, their parents, and the faculty of each KIPP school choose to participate in the program. No one is assigned or forced to attend a KIPP school. Everyone must make and uphold a commitment to the school and to each other to put in the time and effort required to achieve success.

More Time
KIPP schools know there are no shortcuts when it comes to success in academics and life. With an extended school day, week, and year, students have more time in the classroom to acquire the academic knowledge and skills that will prepare them for competitive high schools and colleges, as well as more opportunities to engage in diverse extra-curricular experiences.

Power to Lead
The principals of KIPP schools are effective academic and organizational leaders who understand that great schools require great school leaders. They have control over their school budget and the personnel they appoint. They are free to swiftly move dollars or make staffing changes, allowing them maximum effectiveness in helping students learn.

Focus on Results
KIPP schools relentlessly focus on high student performance on standardized

tests and other objective measures. Just as there are no shortcuts, there are no excuses. Students are expected to achieve a level of academic performance that will enable them to succeed at the nation's best high schools and colleges.

Nearing the school, I started my morning briefing regarding the school, the local area and the school's pedagogical approaches. We agreed that the lines of enquiry on our final day would be the success of the model in developing student aspirations for college entry, the quality of the teaching and resulting outcomes, teacher workload and turnover, student dropout rates and their possible causes.

The first thing we noticed as we entered the school was the now-famous KIPP mantra – 'Work hard. Be nice'. Simplicity in itself but meaningful – hard work, good manners and show respect! The receptionist accompanied us to the school dining room where the teachers and students were gathering. Four things were immediately noticeable on route, and chimed with our visits to the two previous schools.

1. The mantra of the school was clearly visible and it was the first thing students passed each morning.

2. Every wall had a motivational poster extolling the virtues of high levels of attendance.

3. There were constant references to the benefits of 'climbing the mountain to college'.

4. Once more, at the side of each classroom door, was a pennant showing the college that the homeroom teacher attended.

However, KIPP had gone one stage further in that on each classroom door was a photocopy of the front cover of the book that the teacher was presently reading. Reminders of the school's mantra – the need for high attendance, the benefits of a college education and the encouragement to read – hit every student before they even entered their classrooms.

It was 7.15am and school did not start until 7.25am, but already the cafeteria was buzzing with young people who had arrived early for breakfast. KIPP obviously believed that young people could not work effectively when hungry.

We stood at the side of the hall watching the students eating. Dave Levin noticed that we had arrived and waved us over. Quickly greeting us, he asked for time to start the school day. At the clap of his hands the cafeteria fell silent. 'Good morning Kippsters,' he said. 'Good morning Mr. Levin,' they chanted in response. 'Let's try a rap,' he suggested. 'Broken brains?' The entire school started to chant together. The message conveyed by the rap was very clear, in that 'broken brains' don't get you into college. Success would only come by fixing your brains at the start of each day and working hard in every lesson. When the rap was finished Levin spoke to his students about attendance. 'OK guys, attendance on Wednesday and Thursday was 97%, that's ex ellent – congratulations – but I know that you can make it 98%! Remember, school starts at 7.25am so that we can start working at 7.30am. Have a great day – work hard and be nice!' At exactly 7.25am, 250 students left the cafeteria and followed their teacher to their homerooms in silent, well-drilled lines. After the students had left we spent some 20 minutes with Levin while he outlined the KIPP philosophy and ethos. Fortunately I had briefed the tour party well and there were no surprises. After the briefing we were invited to drop into classrooms – as the school had an open door policy – but, once again, we were asked not to disturb students who were on task. We split into pre-arranged groups and started our classroom visits.

In the first room my group entered was a class of nine-year-olds who were reading their set text. Every student had a ruler on the textbook and was moving it slowly down the page as the teacher, walking around the class, carefully ensured that each of her students was following line by line, and reading aloud. I glanced at a whiteboard at the front of the class where the lesson objectives for the first hour's learning were displayed. The bottom objective immediately caught my eye: 'To continue to practise the rules of conversation by using only whole-sentence answers.' I had not seen such an objective before but it clearly reflected the good practice we had seen on the previous two days. After a few minutes the teacher paused and asked a pupil to carry on reading aloud for the next two paragraphs. She repeated this process for about three pages before stopping the class. Glancing around the class, she asked who could summarise, in whole sentences, how the plot was developing. A flurry of hands were raised. The student selected to answer started by responding 'I think that the plot is beginning to…' and began to outline her answer in whole sentences. After she had finished, the teacher looked around the class and selected another pupil. 'Santiago,' she asked 'Do you agree with Maria? 'to which Santiago replied 'I agree with Maria because…', once again using a whole sentence to outline the reason why he agreed. Turning to a third pupil, the teacher then asked if he had anything to add. He responded 'While I agree with Santiago and Maria, I think that they should also consider…'. Having solicited their views, the class started to read once again. Although I had been teaching for many years, I had not seen such precise drilling of conversational techniques. Being able to reply in such a constructed manner would not only build their confidence in terms of conversing with one another, but it would also improve their grammar and word power. More food for thought.

Our next classroom visit was to a class beginning a mathematics lesson. It was a third grade (eight-year-olds) class and their opening task was to put their hands on their desks, palms down, and 'skip chant' their four times table as a class. In low voices they began to chant '4, 8, 12, 16, 20…' and so on, until they reached 48. Having completed the task, the teacher applauded the class and asked them if they could manage it backwards. Together, the class reversed the procedure – '48, 44, 40…' – until they reached where they had started. This was followed with a tables challenge where each student was required to pick another pupil and ask them to 'skip chant' another times table. The exercise produced much fun and each correct chant was rewarded with applause and high fives. After ten minutes of skip chanting, the class settled down into a worksheet of times tables' multiplication questions. While the pupils were working I asked the teacher why the students had started the lesson with their palms on the table. She explained that she did not want anyone trying to count with their fingers. When I asked why not, she quite rightly pointed out how much time is wasted in mathematics examinations by the lack of memorised tables forcing pupils to resort to counting on their fingers. Reflecting back, I knew that I had witnessed many secondary school classes in England where pupils still needed to use their fingers to calculate. Throughout the morning, in class after class, we watched talented teachers drilling their students with the knowledge and skills that would be needed to pass the college entry examinations.

Later in the morning we had a chance to meet the assistant principal to feedback on what we had seen. We were very complimentary about the students' behaviour and the tightness of the classroom and transition routines. He responded by saying that there was a view, outside of the school, that the discipline was too heavy, but he firmly believed that young children needed strong boundaries to guide their energies and efforts. He pointed out that many students, unfortunately, came from troubled or dysfunctional families and that strong routines and codes of conduct helped them to develop the strength of character to concentrate their energies on becoming 'college ready'. He was asked about teacher workload and readily admitted that it was very high. He thought that the average teacher worked some 60 to 80 hours each week and that there was a fair amount of teacher turnover each year. When pushed on the number of students who were successfully entering college, he told us that nationally only 40% of students from low-income backgrounds matriculate to college. KIPP had set a national target of 75% for all KIPP schools and the KIPP Bronx was over 80%. We asked if the intake was better than other schools, but he reminded us that admission was by lottery, although he accepted that there could be students who persuaded their parents not to enter their names in the lottery as they did not like the discipline, longer hours and compulsory homework. This could, he admitted, increase the chances of the more aspirational parents gaining a place for their child. He did accept that there was a small number of students who could not cope with the 'high expectations and no excuses' approach and left within two years of gaining a place, but that the number was in single figures.

At the end of our meeting he told us that a special treat had been arranged to end our visit. Wednesday was usually reserved for orchestra practice but we were to have the opportunity to listen to the school orchestra before the end of our visit. He explained that every pupil in the school was being taught to read and play music and that learning an instrument was a compulsory part of the curriculum. The reasoning behind this decision was not just to build a good school orchestra, but also to prove to the pupils that constant practice can hone skills and improve performance. This was a message that was constantly reinforced in all of the lessons we had visited. I have to admit that everyone in our party was lost for words as we listened in silence to the school orchestra. Like everything we had seen that morning it was a well-disciplined, high-quality performance.

On the coach back to the hotel there was general agreement about the high quality we had witnessed in the final visit of our study tour and KIPP's ability to smash the college admission glass ceiling but also, especially from the residency heads, some doubts about the transferability of its pedagogical practice to the English system. However, there was a general consensus that it would probably work in a 'start-up' school but, in 2008, they were few and far between.

Before getting off the coach I reminded the Future Leaders' participants that they were to work in groups and prepare presentations about their learning, either that afternoon or early Saturday morning, and that these presentations would be commented on by the residency headteachers.

The form below is a sample copy of the KIPP Commitment to Excellence

KIPP Commitment to Excellence   *Work hard. Be nice.*

Teachers' Commitment

We fully commit to KIPP in the following ways:
- We will arrive at KIPP every day by 7:15am (Monday-Friday).
- We will remain at KIPP until 5:00pm (Monday -Thursday) and 4:00pm on Friday.
- We will come to KIPP on appropriate Saturdays at 9:15am and remain until 1:05pm.
- We will teach at KIPP during the summer.
- We will always teach in the best way we know how and we will do whatever it takes for our students to learn.
- We will always make ourselves available to students and parents, and address any concerns they might have
- We will always protect the safety, interests, and rights of all individuals in the classroom.
- Failure to adhere to these commitments can lead to our removal from KIPP.

Signed: ....

Parents'/Guardians' Commitment

We fully commit to KIPP in the following ways:
- We will make sure our child arrives at KIPP by 7:25am (Monday-Friday) or boards a KIPP bus at the scheduled time.
- We will make arrangements so our child can remain at KIPP until 5:00pm (Monday - Thursday) and 4:00pm on Friday.
- We will make arrangements for our child to come to KIPP on appropriate Saturdays at 9:15am and remain until 1:05pm.
- We will ensure that our child attends KIPP summer school.
- We will always help our child in the best way we know how and we will do whatever it takes for him/her to learn. This also means that we will check our child's homework every night, let him/her call the teacher if there is a problem with the homework, and try to read with him/her every night.
- We will always make ourselves available to our children and the school, and address any concerns they might have. This also means that if our child is going to miss school, we will notify the teacher as soon as possible, and we will carefully read any and all papers that the school sends home to us.
- We will allow our child to go on KIPP field trips.
- We will make sure our child follows the KIPP dress code.
- We understand that our child must follow the KIPP rules so as to protect the safety, interests, and rights of all individuals in the classroom. We, not the school, are responsible for the behaviour and actions of our child.
- Failure to adhere to these commitments can cause my child to lose various KIPP privileges and can lead to my child returning to his/her home school.

Signed: ....

Student's Commitment

I fully commit to KIPP in the following ways:
- I will arrive at KIPP every day by 7:25am (Monday-Friday) or board a KIPP bus at the correct time.
- I will remain at KIPP until 5:00pm (Monday - Thursday) and 4:00pm on Friday.
- I will come to KIPP on appropriate Saturdays at 9:15am and remain until 1:05pm
- I will attend KIPP during summer school.
- I will always work, think, and behave in the best way I know how, and I will do whatever it takes for me and my fellow students to learn. This also means that I will complete all my homework every night, I will call my teachers if I have a problem with the homework or a problem with coming to school, and I will raise my hand and ask questions in class if I do not understand something.
- I will always make myself available to parents and teachers, and address any concerns they might have. If I make a mistake, this means I will tell the truth to my teachers and accept responsibility for my actions.
- I will always behave so as to protect the safety, interests, and rights of all individuals in the classroom. This also means that I will always listen to all my KIPP teammates and give everyone my respect.
- I will follow the KIPP dress code.
- I am responsible for my own behaviour, and I will follow the teachers' directions.
- Failure to adhere to these commitments can cause me to lose various KIPP privileges and can lead to returning to my home school.

Signed: ....

On the Saturday morning, I joined the residency headteachers for our first breakfast at a civilised time since the study tour had started. We all agreed that it had been a great visit, in that we had learned a lot about practice in good charter schools and we were looking forward to the four groups of Future Leaders reporting back to us. At 10.30am, we entered the hotel conference room to find our eager aspirant heads, all 'booted and suited', waiting to present to us.

Their presentations were high in quality and reflective in deciding how much of their learning could be transferred to English schools. At the end of each group presentation the residency headteachers asked probing questions to check their Future Leaders' understanding of what they had learned on the study tour.

When the exercise had been completed, I summarised the principal points that had been made by the Future Leaders regarding the similarities that all three charter schools had that were contributing to their success.

1.   A strong moral purpose

Before the charter schools opened, each of the areas that they were to serve had what could only be described as 'broken' education systems that were rife with underachievement. The banning of segregation in American schools had led to 'white flight' from many areas, leaving most schools with African-American and Latino-Hispanic populations. The outcomes of these schools lagged way behind their white counterparts, resulting in a distinct achievement gap. The founders of each of the schools we had visited had a strong moral purpose in seeking to close that gap.

2.   A strong sense of mission

In applying to open such schools, each sponsor had to write a charter for submission to the district education board. The mission of all three schools was both ambitious and aspirational, in that it committed the school to ensuring all of their students passed the college entrance examination. This mission allowed the school leaders to align all staff to focus their energies on the fulfilment of the mission.

3.   Finding and developing the right leaders

All three of the schools we visited were mission driven in nature and had mission-driven people leading them. If these schools were to expand as a movement then they would have to emulate New Leaders and devise ways of producing a pipeline of future leaders.

4.   Instituting strong social norms to develop social capital and character

Social norms are the rules of behaviour that are considered acceptable within a society. Schools with strong social norms would have strong routines and codes of behaviour. These would be seen as essential character building tools that would help their students develop character traits such as determination, tenacity, resilience and grit, and help them achieve the goal of becoming 'college ready'. Each KIPP school had clear procedures and routines for just about everything, from arriving early each morning, to moving in the hallways, to behaving in class, to responding to teachers, and so on. However, these routines and codes were not draconian in nature but made enjoyable by incentivised reward schemes.

5. Teacher belief

In all three schools, we had witnessed total teacher belief in the ability of their students to succeed. Teachers in these schools were continually passing that belief on to their students so as nurture a positive attitudes in tackling challenging learning.

6. A rigorous curriculum model to enhance intellectual capital

Each school had devised a curriculum model that started with the end result in mind. They knew when they needed to have their students college ready and worked backwards in determining the knowledge content that had to be mastered by the end of each grade. Success in one grade became the foundation for additional success in the following grade. Year-on-year, the intellectual and knowledge capital of their students was being carefully developed to ensure college readiness.

7. Regular systematic assessment

In each key area, weekly quizzes were used to check academic progress and understanding. The outcomes of these quizzes identified which individual students needed intervention, support or additional time. They also became an additional tool to identify which areas of teaching were not effective thus allowing additional teacher coaching to take place.

8. A fierce focus on attendance

In all three schools, time in class was viewed as being sacred. If students were not in school, then they were not learning. If they were not learning, they would not become college ready. In order for their mission of 100% of students becoming 'college ready', all three schools set attendance goals of 97% and had distinct rapid response strategies for contacting parents as soon as an unexplained absence was detected. When a student's attendance began to falter, intervention and support strategies were immediately applied.

9. A longer school day

All three charter schools had a longer school day than English schools. This allowed more time for learning as well as creating more opportunities for individual student intervention and support, thus maximising progress on the road to becoming 'college ready'.

In bringing the study tour to a close, I reminded everybody of the words of Martin Luther King when he said that young people should not be judged by the colour of their skin but by the content of their character, and that the development of 'intelligence' and 'character' should be the true purpose of education. I also asked them to reflect on the aspirational names of the charter chains. Amistad was an Achievement First school and that placed achievement of their students at the heart of all of their actions. KIPP was about helping young people recognise the power of knowledge acquisition to help them climb the mountain to college, while North Star was about each young person finding their own North Star to guide them towards becoming 'college ready'. What we had seen was so different from the schools we worked in back in England.

In England, while all schools were now highly accountable for student outcomes, they were not accountable for the next steps in their students' educational career. We had a national curriculum and were hell bent on coverage rather than depth. We spent most of our energy on Key Stage 4. As a result, in too many schools, Key Stage 3 had become the forgotten years instead of the wonder years where we should be developing both intellect and character and emphasising mastery rather than assigning a grade.

It was important, I told them, that if Future Leaders was to become a transformational leadership programme, then each Future Leader had to find their own North Star in determining their personal mission and use the knowledge and learning that they had acquired over the last three days to think through the academic and cultural blueprint of the successful school they would one day lead. There were glass ceilings back in England that were preventing social mobility and they needed breaking, just as the schools we had visited were breaking the glass ceiling to college.

Reflections from the First Study Tour

The philosophy underpinning all three schools was based on a simple premise. If you can get your students emotionally engaged with the school and its teachers, then they feel safe and develop a sense of belonging. This sense of belonging then starts to modify their behaviours, encouraging self-discipline and eliminating negative behaviour traits. Getting the emotional and behavioural engagements right leads to enhanced cognitive engagement which, in turn, produces breakthrough outcomes.

Emotional engagement

Conversations with young people who have dropped out of school often include phrases such as 'I was bored' or 'I couldn't see the point of what they were making us learn'. They had become disengaged with the learning process because they could not see its relevance. School engagement, or the extent to which students are involved in, attached and committed to the academic and social activities in school, plays a prominent role in preventing academic failure, promoting competence, and influencing a wide range of adolescent outcomes. All three of the schools we had visited had worked on ensuring their students knew and understood what their school was trying to achieve for them. Young children in North Star, when asked the question 'Where are you going?' chanted in unison 'To go to college and follow my dream!' The visual displays in each of the schools were strong in terms of emotional engagement by continually encouraging the achievement of the dream. Very early on in each child's educational career, they became emotionally engaged with their school because they understood and bought into its mission and were following their dream.

Behavioural engagement

There is much evidence that reducing challenging behaviour in schools can have a direct and lasting effect on students' learning and their resulting outcomes. All three academies had analysed the roots of misbehaviour in schools and had developed strong routines and boundaries to discourage poor behaviour. Time was the driver behind these routines and all of their students were taught from an early age that every minute spent on learning was a minute bought towards achieving their college dream. They were taught that good routines improved learning time and they believed in the rationale underpinning the routines. Lining up in the schoolyard or cafeteria meant that everyone arrived at class on time and no learning minutes were lost. Passing out books and papers quickly and efficiently bought more time for following the college dream. Routines were made fun and enjoyable and used as an enhancement of the learning process and not a distraction to it. Obviously, these routines did not modify the behaviour of all students and there were the occasional need for correction. KIPP had a 'broken window' approach to poor behaviour interfering with the learning process. They believed that any misbehaviour unaddressed would increase the likelihood of repetition and distract other students from their learning. Each misdemeanour was acted upon quickly and consistent sanctions were applied.

Good school leaders recognise that strong routines and structures liberate learning and enhance student outcomes.

Cognitive engagement

There is no agreement in the research literature as to what motivates learners to engage, but the dominant view is that students engage when they are working towards achieving goals that are meaningful to them. This engagement is increased when they start to believe that they can face up to learning that seems initially challenging and that failure is part of their learning journey on the road to success. The teachers in each of the three schools had a deep belief that, irrespective of educational starting points, previous track record or mother tongue, their students had potential and you just had to get them believing in themselves. They continually passed their belief in each student's ability to succeed onto their students helping them to develop a growth mindset in terms of personal self-belief and future success.

Academic rigour

In any school, there are students who are apprehensive of an academic challenge because they do not want to struggle or fail when they try something new, harder, and more rigorous. The fear of failure in front of their peer group, and possible humiliation, often leads to them giving up and finding a reason not to be in the classroom. This often results in enhanced poor behaviour in the hope that they will be sent outside. Our challenge as educators is to get them to engage in the challenge while being scared of failure, but having the courage to try. They need to understand that we all struggle and fail when we try something new and that we learn new ways to modify what we are doing until we succeed.

Academic rigour is about pitching the learning objectives of each lesson high, identifying where additional support is needed and scaffolding down until each student successfully moves out of their comfort zone and achieves the required level of learning. It is about setting high standards for all and supplying the additional time and support to make sure everyone reaches that high standard. It is about accepting that good differentiation is about additional time and support and not weaker content and lower expectations. The old concept of 'all will, most will, some will' provides a perfect teacher-led excuse for many students not to be rigorous in trying to achieve high goals.

It is the creation of a culture in which each student is expected to learn at high levels, receives supported in achieving those high levels and can demonstrate a thorough, in-depth mastery of the required learning. This results in the development of enhanced cognitive skills such as reflective thought and strategic reasoning. Lessons that are academically rigorous will deliberately encourage problem-solving, thus ensuring the use of critical, analytical and complex lateral thinking. It is about increasing the cognitive load that enables our students to make that jump from passive to dynamic learning.

2008:
New York (again)

Exactly 12 months later, I was back in New York leading another study tour consisting of the third cohort of Future Leaders and their residency headteachers. None of the participants had seen a high-performing charter school in action and I was hoping for the same reactions as I had observed among the participants of the previous year's tour. However, while the group were involved in lesson observations at the three schools, I wanted to spend that time digging deeper into the reasons that underpinned each school's success.

On the previous visit we kept coming across the same two words which, in 2008, were not commonly used by English school leaders. These were '**culture**' and '**climate**'. In England, we talked about a school's ethos rather than culture and climate and I saw this as somewhat of a nebulous term that was used to try to describe what a school stood for. Phrases often appeared in school prospectuses such as 'we have an ethos of high expectations' or 'we have a distinct ethos built on very positive relationships and a desire to develop a love of learning in our students'. These look laudable in print but are often difficult to feel or sense once inside the school.

Researching ethos, culture and climate before the visit I came across a paper by presented by Caitlin Donnelly to the British Educational Research Association Annual Conference in 1999 in which she reproduced a Dancy quote where he provided a useful insight on the concept of school ethos while commenting on Rutter's excellent study '15,000 hours' . He analysed it in terms of values, aims, attitudes and procedures and suggested that 'values order aims, aims inspire attitudes, attitudes issue in, and are exemplified by, actions'. In other words, strong living values could not only guide the direction of a school but could also influence the attitudes, decisions and actions of both teachers and their students.

Looking more deeply into culture I found a definition from 1999 where Prosser had argued that

> 'School culture is an unseen, and unobservable force behind school activities, a unifying theme that provides meaning, direction, and mobilisation for school members. It has both concrete representation in the form of artefacts and behavioural norms, and sustained implicitly by jargon, metaphors and rites.'

Prosser 1999, p.13

However, I would argue that the culture I had seen on my previous visit was visible and deeply entrenched. You could see it in the strong routines that guided behaviour, in the interactions between people, the manner in which the values permeated everybody's actions and the high aspirations of the students.

Empirically grounded school climate research did not really begin until the 1960s, when Halpin and Croft (1963) initiated a study of the impact of school climate on student learning and development. Since then, there has been an extraordinary, growing body of research that attests to the importance of school climate in supporting learning and enhancing outcomes. The research suggests that school leaders, if they want to maximise student outcomes, should pay as much attention to noise levels in corridors and dining rooms, the physical comfort levels of the building, how safe their students feel and the quality of student–teacher interactions, as they do to the quality of teaching in the classroom. Reflecting back on the practices of schools in England, I wondered if 'climate walks' should accompany learning walks. How are parents and visitors greeted when they arrive at the school office? How are they responded to on the telephone? When you watch classroom transitions, are they brief with a sense of purpose or are they times for students to socially interact? If students consider social interaction more important than getting to the next lesson, then they are failing to understand the need to maximise their learning time if they are to succeed in external examinations. When you visit classrooms can you detect a sense of studiousness and desire to achieve or is there chaos and lack of focus? The three schools I had visited the previous year all had very positive cultures and climates. I was determined to try to find out how these had been determined and maintained, as well as how new staff, students and parents were inducted into and aligned with them. Each school was generous in allowing me time with a senior member of staff to patiently help me deepen my understanding of both culture and climate.

In 2008, many charter schools were in their infancy and were operating what is known as a 'K–8' model. They took children in to their kindergarten at the age of four, from where they then transition to elementary school at six years of age and remain in the school until they become 'high school ready' by the age of 14. On our study tours we had always tried to concentrate on the 11–14 age range, where possible, as we thought that this would be more relevant to our Future Leaders' participants who were all working in English secondary schools. However, my conversations in all three schools focused on getting the culture and climate right in kindergarten if long-term success was to be achieved.

School culture
Although I had conversations with each of the deans in three different schools, they all made the same point as to why their specific culture had been created. Each dean pointed out that their charter school was 'mission driven' with the specific goal of getting their students 'high school ready' by the end of Grade 8. Many of these students arrived with low reading and number scores and, if these were to be successfully built upon, then the schools had to create a culture of high aspirations in which every minute of learning time counted. Every action in each of the schools was focused on this aim because, as I was continually told, 'you cannot afford to waste a single minute if you are going to get them college ready!' Pushing harder, I asked how straight lines and silent transitions increased classroom learning time. It was gently pointed out to me that the silent lines meant everyone arrived at class at the same time leaving no stragglers dawdling down the hallway and it allowed a quick, quiet entry to the classroom, where learning could immediately commence. In most classrooms back in England it would often take a good two minutes to get everyone in and settled and that did not include waiting for the odd straggler. If you taught such a class twice per week, then you were losing at least four minutes of learning time each week or two and a half hours per year which was effectively a week's lessons lost. Taken over the five years of secondary education this is 12-and-a-half-hours lost, which is about the same amount of time that many teachers back in England were giving to Year 11 during their supposed holidays to maximise their students' outcomes.

Why strong living values are important
Each of the three schools had their own set of values that were embedded in their culture and guided their decisions and actions. They were not pious words painted on a wall or printed in a prospectus but were the lingua-franca of the

charter school. Unsurprisingly, there were several values common to each school.

- Achievement, in that all were focused on ensuring that as many students as possible were college ready at the end of their elementary school career.
- Integrity, in that each school had strong moral principles and would always be honest with teachers regarding their classroom performance and how the school could help improve it. When necessary, each school was honest with students and their parents as to the progress they were making as they 'climbed the mountain to college'.
- Perseverance, as in the need for grit, hard work and never giving up if the students' ascent to college was to be successful.
- Respect for their teachers and the commitment they were making to help the journey, respect for learners, in that they should not have their learning disturbed, and respect for their environment which had been deliberately designed to encourage aspiration.

Classroom visits showed that all teachers constantly used the values to reinforce the character traits that they were trying to develop in their students. Never would you hear a student being praised for being intelligent or clever. Such praise would send a strong message that ability governed progress. It was the deed, not the person that had to be complimented so as to continually reinforce those essential character traits.

Finding the right teachers

Each school website contained similar exhortations in their drive to find the right teachers for their schools.

'Great teachers and staff make great schools. Teachers, administrators and staff are on the frontline of education every day. They are the lifeblood of what makes our school special and successful. We are always looking for innovative and inspiring teachers to join us. Choosing to be part of our family in supporting young people on their journey to college is the decision of a lifetime. Apply now.'

Such adverts are more emotional than factual and are of deliberate intent. Emotional marketing is deliberately focused on the ego of the reader. Careful phraseology seeks out mission-driven teachers.

- Great teachers and staff make great schools – only great teachers and staff should apply here.

- Staff are on the frontline of education every day – come and be part of our revolution.
- They are the lifeblood of what makes the school special and successful – you will be become indispensable to our mission.
- Choosing to be part of our family – you will not be left alone in the classroom as you will always be part of our family.
- Supporting young people on their journey to college is the decision of a lifetime – you could not get a better closing line in seeking mission-driven people.

By using such emotive advertising you are clearly laying out your mission and culture and showing candidates the character traits you will be trying to identify in the selection process.

The selection process used by one of the principals was very 'left field' in the sense that it certainly did not fit the usual application, shortlist, demonstration lesson and interview you would find at home. She was determined to find teachers whose personal values were already close to those of the school, in the knowledge that appointing anyone whose values were not aligned could easily distort the mission. Following the letter of application, each applicant would be phoned at home during the evening by the principal. The conversation would not follow the usual 'tell me why you have applied' route but would concentrate on the personal qualities and character strengths of the applicant. Well-meaning applicants would sometimes mirror those of the school in making an application but the principal wanted to dig behind the rhetoric and test the applicants' stated values to see if they were deeply held. If the telephone conversation was successful then the principal would invite the applicant to a downtown coffee shop, usually hidden well away. Why? If the application was serious then the applicant would demonstrate good planning and time management skills by getting to the well-hidden coffee shop on time.

Having passed the first two stages of the selection process, the applicant would be invited to give a demonstration lesson in the principal's school. The letter of invitation would ask the candidate to arrive an hour early so that they could collect current student progress data regarding the class they were to teach and have time to plan the lesson. The principal did not want to see a well-rehearsed lesson delivered, but one that reflected the progress each pupil had already made. After the lesson, the participant would be given feedback and invited to deliver the lesson again. High-quality coaching and feedback was an important part of the culture of the school and the principal wanted to see how receptive the applicant was to feedback. The final part of the process was the personal interview. At the end of the whole process the panel was not asked if the candidate was appointable, but instead what – in terms of values, mission, attitude and pedagogical practice – the school would have to work on to make them an excellent teacher. They were prepared to work with all of their appointees on the journey to excellent teaching but the starting point had to be alignment with the school's mission and values if she was to become 'one of the family'. Cultural alignment was the most prominent part of the process.

Inducting new teachers into the culture

In 2008, induction for new teachers in English schools was simply a matter of turning up at the start of term, meeting everybody and getting your new classroom ready before your students arrive. If you were very lucky you might be visited by your head of year or spend some time with your head of department learning about the school's expectations. In all of the three schools we visited, induction was not simply seen as a day's activity but the start of a much longer journey about building each teacher's beliefs and expertise so that they have a greater long-term impact on their student's learning. The enthusiasm of new teachers does not always equate with confidence and professional understanding. They may believe that they can make a difference to each students' life, but they do not readily arrive with the diverse range of skills needed to instantly and successfully manage their classrooms. Although they may have some awareness of the school culture they are about to enter, they will be unaware of the routines and rituals that support this culture. All three schools we visited firmly believed that each new teacher had to be given sufficient induction time to develop the correct mindset, learn, practise and refine the routines and procedures that the maintenance of the already-successful culture would need, and develop the classroom skills that a successful teacher needs.

The American Dream is a national ethos which includes the belief that prosperity, success and upward social mobility can be achieved through hard work. Teachers in these charter schools had their own version of the American Dream, in that they held a universal belief that all students can be destined for success when each teacher has a deep belief that all of their students have endless potential and they, as teachers, have the ability and skills to help them along the road to fulfilling it. The logic of their argument was simple: if the teacher has the right mindset and continually passes this unfailing belief on to her students then the mindset of the students will change as they gain the personal belief that they can improve, and this change in mindset will change their actions and endeavours in the classroom as they 'climb the mountain to college'.

Rookie induction was meticulously planned and would last at least two weeks before the students returned to school. As part of their induction, rookie teachers would be taken through the work of Robert Rosenthal and Leonora Jacobson from 1963 when they visited a public elementary school in California and persuaded the teachers there that they had devised an intelligence test called the 'Harvard Test of Inflected Acquisition' which would identify students who could be expected to be 'growth spurters' that year. Having administered the test, Rosenthal and Jacobson simply filed it away without marking it. After a short time they returned to the school and identified, without evidence, a group of students that could be expected to be 'growth spurters' that year. What the teachers did not know was that these 'growth spurters' were chosen at random. On returning to the school at the end of the academic year, the researchers were told by the teachers that the test was an excellent predictor of academic growth, as all of the students they had identified had improved during the year far more than their peers, thus confirming Rosenthal and Jacobson's belief that teacher's beliefs and expectations had a great influence on student outcomes.

They would also look at the work of Carol Dweck, a Professor of Psychology at Stanford University. In her book *Mindset: The New Psychology of Success*, published in 2006, she outlined a belief that individuals can be placed on a continuum according to their implicit views of where ability comes from. Those who believed that success was based on innate ability were said to have a 'fixed' mindset, while others who believed that success is based on hard work, learning, repeated practice and perseverance have a 'growth' mindset. Individuals with a fixed mindset dread failure as, believing that intelligence is fixed, they perceived it as a negative statement regarding their basic ability. On the other hand, individuals with a growth mindset saw failure as a learning experience on the road to success. One of her most significant quotes was:

> *'In a fixed mindset students believe their basic abilities, their intelligence, their talents, are just fixed traits. They have a certain amount and that's that, and then their goal becomes to look smart all the time and never look dumb. In a growth mindset students understand that their talents and abilities can be developed through effort, good teaching and persistence. They don't necessarily think everyone's the same or anyone can be Einstein, but they believe everyone can get smarter if they work at it.'*

Carol Dweck on the Growth Mindset and Education
OneDublin.org, 2012-06-19

All of the charter schools had a distinct vision of success in terms of maximising the number of students who would become college ready before leaving them.

To achieve this success they had to develop a culture based on the belief that intelligence was malleable and that, by developing a growth mindset in their teachers, they would, in turn, foster growth mindsets in their students. I cannot recollect 'mindset' being part of the induction programme of any newly qualified teacher in a school in England in 2008 or even part of the NPQH leadership programme.

After mindsets, the training turned to the establishment of fixed routines and rituals that would modify student behaviour, producing a positive climate for learning. All three schools had their own approaches but, once again, there was a similarity in practice. Silent line-ups were considered an essential first step in establishing good behaviour before a classroom was entered. Each rookie teacher was taught how to quickly establish this practice and, dependent on the grade they were to teach, the songs and raps which would make the learning of the line-up fun. They were taught how to lead this line-up walking backwards so that they could always ensure the line was straight and mouths were closed. As part of the training, they had to play the part of students at lunchtime, learning how important good manners are in terms of saying 'please' and 'thank you' when choosing and collecting food in the cafeteria, as well as the good table manners that were expected while eating. Many classroom routines – from how students enter the classroom, to how they would store their bags before sitting, to how an effective morning circle should be organised, to the speedily handing out of paper in a more senior classroom, so as to maximise learning time – would be continually practised so that when the rookies eventually entered their own classroom they would not only be confident practitioners well versed in the charter schools routines and rituals but would be fully immersed in the school's high expectations culture.

In terms of classroom practice, all rookie teachers would spend their first week sat at the back of the classroom of a veteran teacher studying how experienced practitioners maximised learning time and established time-saving and behavioural-conditioning routines. At the end of each day, they met with the dean of instruction (teaching and learning coach) to discuss their observations and new learning.

The induction process was both meticulous and thorough. It was delivered with the express intention of ensuring that all rookie teachers became well-immersed in the high-expectations culture of the school, and was light-years ahead of any practice I had seen back home.

Aligning parents with the schools' culture
Sometime after the awarding of a place by lottery, and before each student

started at school, the family was visited by a senior member of the school to start the alignment process. Each visit followed a well-orchestrated script which commenced with the member of staff outlining the benefits of a successful college education in terms of financial security and upward social mobility, but also stressing the amount of hard work that would be expected from both the child and their family if college were to be accessed.

The commitments of the school to the child and her family were carefully explained in terms of the schools' mission, culture and values, punctuality, attendance, the amount of homework that would be set, the high expectations that would be continually enforced, the need for strong routines and the sanctions that would be applied if progress was not being made. This would not be delivered in either a tough or threatening manner, but as a gentle and careful explanation of what the school would need to do if the child was to become college ready. By explaining all of this before entry there could be little comeback as the academic year started when parents saw at first hand the schools' methodology. This was then followed by asking each parent to support the schools' efforts by guaranteeing high levels of attendance, checking the quality of homework each evening, listening to their child read each night before going to bed, ensuring uniform is checked before their child sets out to school and attending all parents' evenings. This would be followed by a conversation with the child where, before their parents, they would promise to be on time for school each day in full uniform, their attendance would be as high as possible, all homework would be completed and they would make their best efforts every day.

When the school representative, the parents and the child were happy with, and accepted, the high-expectations culture, all parties would sign a commitment contract which would signal the start of the child's charter school education.

Aligning students with the school culture

At the start of each academic year, all new students spend their initial week being inducted into, and aligned with, the high-expectations culture of the school. All other grades have a shorter realignment period but culture is the priority at the start of each year.

The alignment practices were well thought out and made relevant to grade age. Early grade induction relied heavily on learning the songs and rhymes that go with each activity, such as the 'Good morning, good morning' to start the day. Higher grades might start with the 'Work hard, get smart' chant but whatever device was used, it was designed to teach a routine that would maximise learning time in the classroom. There were fixed routines to be learned for entering school, entering the classroom, getting your equipment ready, and so on. Teacher signals were learned for 'stop and listen' as well as 'stop talking'. In higher grades the realignment process would consist of reminders of how to set out your work in your folder, the importance of neatness, and how to put your hand up to answer a question. Throughout the induction period there was great emphasis on the development of good classroom etiquette. No matter what was being taught during this introductory period, the same steps were being followed by each teacher in each classroom.

The process consisted of the following six simple steps.

1. Begin with the end in mind by knowing what perfection would look like when the class had perfected the routine.

2. Model the activity to your students several times. If you want them to line up quietly then, having asked them to watch you, walk across the classroom in silence and stand quietly facing the door.

3. Now get a small group of students to demonstrate the routine to you and the class.

4. Slowly increase the number of students until the whole class is following the routine.

5. Now introduce a timer to see how fast the class can successfully complete the whole routine.

6. Remember that routines are best learned when they are fun.

A skilled veteran teacher would, after the routine had been learned and well-honed, ask the class to tell him what he was doing wrong as he purposefully failed to complete the routine properly. No matter how experienced or inexperienced the teacher was, the process was simple – model, practise, repeat, refine and celebrate.

School climate

It was the collective opinion of all three deans that I met during the study tour that if students feel connected to their school, then they are able to develop positive relationships with the adults in the school and that this, in turn, helped them develop positive behaviours and avoid behaviours that are antisocial. They stressed that, in ensuring a positive climate was developed, senior staff worked hard in only recruiting staff who believed that at all students can succeed and were prepared to go the extra mile in dedicating their time in helping students to fulfil their potential and supplying the necessary emotional support when it was needed. They were confident that each of their schools had a positive climate with an observable ethos that encouraged rigour and hard work, the development of strong positive and respectful relationships between students and their teachers, fair and consistent policies that place rewards before sanctions and a moral environment that promoted values, ethical behaviour and character building.

They stressed that it was the role of the school leaders to promote a positive climate and that this could be achieved by:.

- having a clear vision for the future of the school and the development of its students
- establishing a set of shared values that supported the vision
- having unceasingly high expectations of both staff and students
- always going the extra mile to provide support for both staff and students so as to ensure that they achieve their aspirations
- ensuring consistent and fair accountability at all levels
- seeing parents as partners and not opponents, and
- devoting much of their time to continually communicating their vision, values and expectations to teachers, students and their parents.

It had been a fascinating and informative three days listening to the three deans outline the manner in which each of their schools had established their high-expectations culture and positive climate and I had learned much more than I expected to learn.

At the time of writing, Ofsted guidance to inspectors regarding the making of final judgements contains such phrases as 'a culture of high expectations', a 'culture of ambitions' and a 'culture of respect and tolerance'. However, in 2008, leaders of schools in England had little knowledge of the enhancing effect a culture of 'high expectations and no excuses', coupled with a positive school climate, could have on student outcomes. If we were to break that glass ceiling in social mobility, especially in challenging urban environments, then we had to fundamentally change our approaches. I reflected on my two previous headships and wondered how much better student outcomes would have been if I had consciously put as much effort into culture and climate as I had put into improving the quality of teaching.

Reflections from the Second Study Tour

I have visited many schools in the 52 years I have been teaching, leading and coaching and have witnessed at first hand the effect of school culture on teachers, students and their parents. Schools with a strong positive culture have highly motivated teachers. Highly motivated teachers have higher levels of enthusiasm and a stronger determination to ensure the long-term success of their students. This enthusiasm rubs off on their students who work harder to achieve success not only for themselves personally but as a form of recognition and thanks for the dedication of their teachers. Schools with a negative, or toxic, culture often contain many cynical teachers who have little belief in their students' ability to succeed.

Good school leaders know that one of the key building blocks in creating a high-performing school is the constant nurturing and maintenance of a high-expectations culture.

School culture
A school's culture is largely determined by the values, shared beliefs and behaviours of all stakeholders within the school community and reflects the school's social norms.

The culture continuum
All school cultures lie on a continuum with positive and toxic at either end. A school with a positive culture has high aspirations for both staff and students, while in a school with a toxic culture you will find students viewed as the problem of all that is wrong in the school with the blame for underperformance being placed squarely on their shoulders.

Aspirational culture

A school which nurtures a sense of aspiration in its students has:

- *a clear vision for student development and progress which is continually communicated to the students*
- *shared values and expectations that support these goals*
- *unceasingly high expectations for its students*
- *individual support mechanisms in place to ensure they achieve the school's aspirations*
- *strategies that show students the possibilities open to them in life and the pathways to those possibilities*
- *strong relationships with parents, seeing them as partners in achieving their child's success*
- *strong and individualised professional development for its staff, to ensure they have the skills to help students achieve their aspirations consistent accountability throughout the school*

Culture is not formed by motivational speeches or the recitation of values, but by repeated practice. Schools with a strong aspirational culture ensure that students receive a continual message that nothing is as important as learning. Every minute of every day is spent on building good habits. Such cultures are created by continually sweating the small stuff – paying full attention to the minutiae. If we concentrate on getting the tiniest of details right then the harder challenges becomes easier.

School values

School values were not as prominent in 2008 as they are today. Nowadays, almost every school website that you visit or prospectus that you open contains a set of laudable values. Unfortunately, far too many of these are laminated or printed rather than lived. A school that has 'living' values ensures that these values permeate the actions and interactions of the day-to-day life of the school.

North Star Academy had adopted the acronym REACH to make their values memorable to the whole-school community. REACH – respect, enthusiasm, achievement, citizenship and hard work – was a fundamental gene in the DNA of the school.

KIPP does not have an easily memorable acronym for students to memorise when adopting the school's values, but students soon see the importance of zest, grit, self-control, optimism, gratitude, social intelligence and curiosity in climbing the mountain to college.

Achievement First had adopted a series of snappy phrases to demonstrate their values. These were 'results without excuses, high expectations, team and family, whatever it takes, many minds one mission and everything with integrity.'

You only had to spend a short time in each school to understand how these were living values. They permeated everything from the displays on the walls to the language of each classroom and the language of the teacher–parent meeting. Living not laminated!

Shared beliefs

The teachers of each school all had a common shared belief that each of their students, irrespective of community environment, educational starting point or mother tongue, had the potential to access college and that their challenge was to ensure that the students had a 'college-focused' attitude and the necessary knowledge, skills and support to get there. They knew that a large part of their task was building the self-belief and self-esteem of their students and that they themselves had to have the right mindset if they were to help them.

The way in which teacher beliefs can enhance student outcomes is illustrated below.

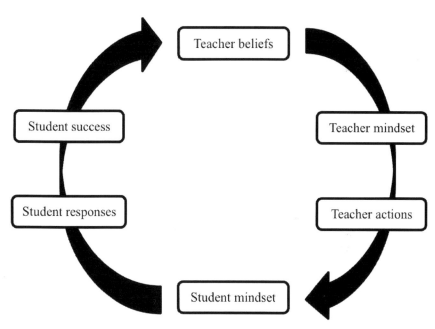

School behaviours

Much of the antisocial behaviour displayed by young people in society can be traced back to the environment in which they are living. Their behaviours are often the result of the influences they have experienced or observed during their development. Many young people who have grown up surrounded by numerous and frequent examples of antisocial behaviour begin to accept it as the norm. Some who have had traumatic family experiences are often scarred and act in antisocial ways as a way of protecting themselves from possible future occurrences of such traumas.

All three schools we visited believed that each student's personal behaviour could be improved by helping them set personal goals and encouraging self-discipline. They saw disruptive behaviour as a reflection of lack of impulse control, self-awareness and positive social habits and that behaviour could be influenced by the schools' own high expectations for self-discipline. They used extensive routines not only to save learning time but to codify behaviours.

Establishing strong routines

Strong routines together with the encouragement of self-discipline and self-reliance develops character in your students and liberates their learning.

Lining up in the playground or cafeteria

The rationale behind establishing this routine is that:

1. *It sets the high-expectations ethos before the classroom is reached.*

2. *It allows the teacher to establish control of the class before entry to the classroom.*

3. *Everybody arrives at the classroom together saving learning time and preventing lesson disruption by stragglers.*

It teaches self-discipline.

Greeting at the classroom door

The rationale behind establishing this routine is that:

1. *It allows each student to be greeted on a personal basis prior to entry.*

2. *It strengthens the emotional relationship between teacher and student.*

3. *It allows the teacher to have a conversation with every student before the lesson commences.*

4. *It allows the teacher to control the entrance routines.*

Seating plans

The rationale behind establishing this routine is that:

1. *They allow the teacher to decide on the most effective way to maximise learning.*

2. *They allow the teacher to arrange the classroom to fit the learning activity.*

3. *They stop the rush for the back row or sitting by the window.*

4. *They prevent student friction as to who sits together.*

5. *They allow the teacher to decide on learning pairs and peer-support strategies.*

Bags and coats

The rationale behind establishing this routine is that it:

1. *Stops bags and coats being placed on tables to produce hiding places.*

2. *Keeps the rows between desks from becoming an obstacle course.*

Equipment ready on desk

This allows the teacher to check that the correct equipment has been brought to the lesson and prevents learning time being interrupted by requests for pens etc.

Do-now

This is a three-to-five minute exercise, executed in silence that commences as soon as each student is seated. It encourages 'bell-to-bell' working, as well as self-discipline by working in silence for the first few minutes of each lesson.

No shouting out answers

By insisting on a 'hands up' approach to answering questions the teacher can:

- *check progress as to how many seem to know the answer*
- *use wait time effectively*
- *control who answers the question.*

Social norms

Social norms are the unwritten rules that govern how we interact with others and our environment. When visiting a school that has adopted a policy of 'protect the planet by not dropping litter' as a norm, you would not expect to see litter in the playground or cafeteria. When a school has a strong positive ethos it usually has strong, unwritten social norms. You would not detect any signs of bullying, homophobic behaviour or gender discrimination, as the students would know from the culture that that was not the expected behaviour. Strong social norms are the acceptance of the schools' unwritten rules such as no skipping to the front in lunch queue, not dropping litter, not invading personal space, being punctual, and so on.

School climate

School climate may be defined as the learning environment and relationships found within a school community. A positive school climate exists when all members of the school community feel safe, included, and accepted, and actively promote positive behaviours and interactions. Positive school climates help develop a culture of mutual respect and are a crucial component in the prevention of inappropriate behaviour.

You can detect the climate of a school by the way the telephone is answered when you ring, how you are greeted on arrival at the school's front desk, the interactions of the teachers and the students in each classroom and the manner in which students interact with each other in corridors, playgrounds and cafeterias.

Schools with positive cultures, positive climates and strong social norms are good places in which to teach and learn, resulting in high student outcomes.

Boston, 2009

Since 2006, Future Leaders had paid for 40 residency school leaders to visit charter schools in the US. This investment was not just a thank you for being a residency school; it was a way of getting the leaders of these schools to understand not only why our leadership training was so different to other programmes, but to help them understand the practices that we wanted our Future Leader residents to hone in their schools. I spent much of April and May that year visiting the residency schools to try to ascertain if having a Future Leader as a year-long resident had impacted on the schools' everyday practices.

I did not have to get as far as a formal interview with the principal to see the effect that the programme was having. Most of the schools were displaying notices stating that they were a 'high expectations and no excuses' school. There were many examples of motivational posters around the school – such as 'Don't count the days – make the days count' and 'Focus on Success' – and classroom doors had signs on them showing which university the teacher had attended. Interviews with the principals showed that the first thing they had tried since the visit was to make the visible culture of the school more aspirational. When I asked about classroom practice, they were still not impressed by the didactic approaches they had seen. I was going to have to dig deeper to see why the charter schools were committed to such a traditional approach.

I deliberately asked if I could lead my third study tour to Boston in order to develop a greater understanding of high schools rather than elementary. The Massachusetts Education Reform Act of 1993 had opened the door for non-profit organisations to apply to open a charter school and, given the 14 years that had passed since then, the charter schools that the study tour was scheduled to visit were more established than those in New York and had both elementary and high school campuses. Once again we were to visit three schools: Boston Collegiate, Roxbury Prep and Excel Academy Charter School. The format of the visit for the new cohort of Future Leaders' participants and their residency school representatives would be the same as on other tours but I had a new sub-agenda. During the spring, I had seen how the culture of the successful charter schools was being replicated back home, but on this visit I wanted to take a deeper look as to how the didactic approach to teaching was helping so many young people break through the glass ceiling to college. I was confident that our visit to Boston was going to be really interesting.

Our first school, Boston Collegiate, had been opened by Bret Peiser and Susan Fortin. Peiser, the son of New York public school teachers, and Fortin had just completed a master's in Public Policy at Harvard Kennedy and they wanted to take advantage of the new freedoms given to education under the Massachusetts' reform act. In applying for permission to open a charter school they described the ethos that they wanted to develop in their school:

> *'We want to reimagine what a school can be. We want to hire the most knowledgeable, the most stimulating, and the most enthusiastic instructors. We want to show students the miraculous features of the natural world and the beauty of writing the perfect sentence. We want students to see not the struggle of the challenge but the pleasure of the struggle. We, as parents, educators, and community members, want to transfer and infuse the love we have for learning to the children of Boston. We want to show kids what school and their future can be and not what it has to be. This is the ethos of our school.'*

In one paragraph they had brought together high-quality, enthusiastic teaching, the love of learning, the necessity of academic rigour and high aspirations.

The second visit on our itinerary was to be Roxbury Prep. The school had opened in Mission Hill, Boston, in 1999. It was founded on the philosophy that all students can succeed in college preparatory programs when they follow a well-planned and engaging curriculum and have support in developing the character strengths needed to work hard enough to access college. The school also had a firm focus on each student developing a strong sense of community responsibility. Curriculum, character and civic responsibility were their 'college-ready' drivers.

Our final visit was to be Excel Academy Charter School. In 2003, Yutaka Tamura founded Excel with a clear vision of creating a public school that would close the educational opportunity gap afflicting the mostly poor, immigrant families living in East Boston and Chelsea, Massachusetts. At that time, the quality of public schooling options available to these young people was much lower than the schools available to their wealthier peers in and outside of Boston. The mission of Excel is *'to prepare students to succeed in high school and college, apply their learning to solve relevant problems, and engage productively in their communities.'*

Once again, the focus was on making students 'college ready' but an additional emphasis was placed on academic rigour and community engagement. Despite only opening in 2003 by 2007 Excel had already been recognised as the 'National Charter School of the Year' by the US Center for Educational Reform.

Once again, I contacted the schools beforehand and explained that I would like to get a better understanding of their teaching model. In particular, I wanted to find out more about how they recruited the right people, how these people were inducted into the school, the thinking behind their classroom practice and how they made these people 'great teachers' who were committed to breaking the glass ceiling to college entry. During the course of the three-day study tour I managed to have lengthy conversations with the school leaders and was able to verify their explanations through ten classroom observations.

Finding the right people

All three charter schools stressed the importance of finding people who were the right fit for the school when filling vacancies. As one dean put it 'you have to see from their application that they have fully researched the school, its mission beliefs and values. Demonstrating alignment is probably the most important first hurdle for all applicants. We are looking for people with one hundred percent commitment to the belief that all students can go to, and graduate from, top colleges.'

The second criteria that the schools looked for was the 'team factor', in that they wanted people who were good team players. Applicants had to demonstrate the capability of becoming a successful member of a hard-edged team determined to help students get into college. 'Mavericks are good,' I was told 'but we have so little time to achieve our goal with each individual student that we see it as a team effort and, because of this, we need good team players. We need dedicated people who are prepared to work as part of a team with common systems, accountability and expectations.'

The third criteria they sought was the applicant's ability to demonstrate a passion for their subject area – geeks and nerds were always welcome! People with a passion for a subject and an unrelenting enthusiasm to pass on that passion made, in their opinion, stimulating teachers. Finally, they wanted people with the ability to self-reflect. They were not looking for the applicant to be the 'finished article'. They firmly believed that with enough coaching and enough development the vast majority of successful applicants would become great teachers. However, for this to work they needed applicants who were reflective practitioners, capable of accepting constructive feedback and possessing the ability to self-reflect on their own practice. To check this quality each applicant had to deliver a sample lesson as part of the interview process. After this had taken place, the principal would give the applicant feedback on the lesson. During this part of the process the principal would be forming an opinion of the applicant's response to the feedback. It was important to all three schools that successful applicants were reflective practitioners who not only were self-critical but could respond positively to feedback. They had to have an inbuilt desire to continually improve their classroom practice.

When asked if the pay scales were an added attraction to work in their schools they readily admitted that the freedom to pay 15% above other schools helped recruitment, but they also pointed out that their teachers worked longer hours and had to come back to school up to three weeks before a new academic year started so as to plan their year-long teaching programme and help induct any newly appointed teachers. They saw the additional pay as a small compensation for these extra hours. When I asked where the additional finance came from, their response was that high-quality teaching was their greatest resource and if paying 'above state' meant the careful management of expenditure on other resources then that was a small price to pay.

Inducting and aligning new staff
Each of the schools brought their teachers back at least two weeks before the state's public schools. This gave them time to induct new teachers into the academic and culture programmes of the school. I have already outlined the emphasis that was placed on cultural alignment and this was matched by an equal emphasis on the pedagogical approaches that the schools had adopted. All three academies had spent several years determining the knowledge and skills that their students would require to pass the college entrance exam and had painstakingly worked backwards to see where each student needed to be at the end of each academic year if they were to be on track to access college at the end of high school. From this information, programmes of study had been produced for each year group, which included assessments and quizzes, each one building on the knowledge and skills acquired in the previous years. Each school, as with every other charter school I had visited had opted for the 'direct instruction' approach to curriculum delivery. It was heavily scripted and nothing had been

left to chance. I was told that to understand why this particular model had been chosen by all of the charter schools, I would need a greater understanding of the 'War on Poverty' initiative of President Lyndon B. Johnson.

In 1967 the Johnson administration, as part of its 'War on Poverty' initiative, began a study of the best teaching models that would close the achievement gap in American schools. Their reasoning was quite simple in that, if they could close the achievement gap, they would have a better-educated workforce who could gain employment and no longer be in poverty. The study, to be called 'Project Follow Through' was carried out by Stanford University and has been cited as the largest controlled study of teaching methodologies with over 200,000 students in 178 communities taking part. Each school in the study was paired with a 'statistical' neighbour. One of the pair was asked to implement one of twelve possible teaching methods, with the statistical neighbour acting as performance comparator. The 12 models ranged from child-centred pedagogical approaches, to Direct Instruction (DI) which involved a teacher-centred approach for training academic skills. A 1977 evaluation of the project involving the use of the Metropolitan Achievement Test, the Coopersmith Self-Esteem Inventory and the Intellectual Achievement Responsibility Scale overwhelmingly favoured DI as the best method of closing the achievement gap. The schools that had adopted this approach were not only outperforming their statistical neighbour but also many of their neighbouring public schools. There was an immediate backlash at the results of the research, with the educational establishment, which was generally in favour of child-centred approaches, rejecting the findings. Supporters of a child-centred or 'progressive' approach attacked the use of sequenced, structured instruction as being insensitive to the needs and interests of the learner and, ultimately, ineffective at promoting true intellectual development. Sadly, this debate still rages today despite little research evidence to support the progressive philosophy.

Direct Instruction (DI)

Child-centred approaches often provide open-ended opportunities for students to explore curriculum material in line with their own interest and aptitude, with the result being that each student becomes responsible for their learning and the level of mastery they wish to achieve. DI adjusts the curriculum, instruction and level of support around each student with the aim that all students experience high levels of success. The responsibility for this success passes from the individual student to the school as it adapts its teaching methods to ensure high-level mastery is achieved by all students.

The curriculum in a DI school is purposefully designed to be presented in a specific sequence so that 'new' knowledge is built upon the review, application and mastery of older knowledge in a manner that is clear, explicit and manageable. The method of instruction is also sequenced to provide a gradual transition from teacher-led to teacher-guided learning and, eventually, independent practice at a high level of mastery.

A typical DI lesson

To many observers a DI lesson would look very traditional in approach and would possibly be viewed as somewhat old fashioned but, for me, the most effective way to judge the effectiveness of any teaching is in the outcomes that it produces.

A typical start to a charter school DI lesson is the customary **meet and greet** entry procedures that ensure emotional and behavioural engagement as soon as the lesson starts. The handshake and personal greeting at the classroom door is the initial emotional engagement and a rigidly enforced seating plan is the start of the behavioural engagement process. As soon as each student sits down they start work on a **do-now** which is a starter exercise designed to ensure that all students are 'learning ready' and that each lesson has 'bell-to-bell' working. The brief five-minute exercise is either linked to previous learning or is designed to reinforce basic skills. As soon as the timed exercise is complete the teacher will commence the **review and preview** stage of the lesson. In this section the previous learning will be revisited and the new learning placed into the context of the old learning, as well as its importance on the 'mountain they are climbing to college'. This is an important stage in the charter school approach to DI. Keeping students enthused and focused on the long-term aim keeps their engagement and strengthens their resolve to succeed. The lesson goals are then clearly articulated and explained so that nobody lacked an understanding of the challenge they were being set. There is no concept of 'all, most, and some'. There is one level of aspiration and it is the teachers' responsibility to ensure that every student reaches that level.

Following the review and preview phase the teacher will move in to **modelling the new learning.** This is done in small stages with each block building of the previous block. As each block unfolds, the teacher will skillfully ask questions to determine each students understanding of the learning. In all of the lessons I observed, I never witnessed the use of closed questions. 'Yes' or 'no' answers were not considered challenging enough if the student was to climb the mountain to college. Random cold calling would be constantly used to ensure whole-class focus. There would always be a measured period of **wait time** after each question had been asked and very rarely would a teacher accept the first answer she would be given. On hearing the answer she would cold call another pupil and ask if the answer was correct or if any further information could be added. All students had to use whole-sentence answers so as to improve their oracy skills and help them gain self-confidence when speaking publicly. Having solicited the correct answer the teacher would always turn to the whole class to ask for a show of hands to see if students agreed with the answer, thus checking on whole-class progress. Quite often, after hands had been held up, the teacher would cold call another pupil to ask why he agreed. Academic rigour in action. The questions were always of a higher order and used both logically and sequentially to gradually enhance the cognitive load, while ensuring academic rigour. Analytical, strategic and critical thinking would be constantly encouraged. This phase would not be ended until the teacher was certain that the students had a confident grasp of the new learning.

Following the modelling of new learning the direct instruction process will move on to a period of **guided practice** where the students will be engaged in practising the learning and applying it in different contexts. During guided practice the teacher will move from student to student giving appropriate feedback, support and additional time where a need is identified.

Towards the end of the lesson the teacher will move the class into the **independent practice phase** where students will work by themselves, gaining further practice so as to move towards mastery. This session will end approximately five minutes before the end of the lesson and the teacher will display an **exit ticket question** on the board. The students will attempt this final question with their books shut so that the teacher can see how much of the learning has been mastered. These tickets are handed in as each student leaves, allowing the teacher to analyse their learning before planning the next lesson.

Throughout the whole lesson an observer would have witnessed strong classroom management with high-quality, well-scripted teaching, moving the learning from passive through active and towards dynamic learning with enthused students producing high outcomes.

I had visited nine charter schools on the three study tours. Each of these schools served communities in which the American Dream was just a dream. Poverty was rife and aspiration was rare. Education, before these schools were founded, was considered broken with far too many young people failing to finish high school. The founding of these schools had started to reverse that trend. Each school was strict with immovable behavioural boundaries. The hours were longer than the neighbouring public schools and the expected standards higher. They were not educational prisons as there was a sense of joy and aspiration in each school. There was a sense of disciplined mission in all that they undertook. They were staffed by disciplined people with disciplined thoughts and disciplined actions, who were there with one intention. That was to break the glass ceiling to college, and they were succeeding.

Reflections on 2009

Mission, vision, values and culture

Each of the successful charter schools had to define their mission, vision, values and culture in their charter application forms before they were allowed to open. Each application form required the applicant to show how the mission and vision would become embedded in the daily life of the school. They had to show how they would use their set of values to guide all of their actions and the culture they would be seeking to establish in their school, as well as the expected outcomes they anticipated.

In 2009, there were less than 200 academies in England, with all other schools firmly under local authority control. It was not a requirement that any school, either academy or local authority controlled, should demonstrate such features.

Finding the right people

In 2009, the recruitment process in England was simple and somewhat linear. Advertise in the Times Educational Supplement inviting applications, read letters of application, shortlist, observe demonstration lesson (usually well practised), interview, and, finally, appoint. The only difference in schools serving challenging urban areas was that they may have to interview two or three times because, often, they were not getting the caliber of applicant that they really needed. Having a system-wide absence of mission, vision, values and culture within our schools, interview questions tended to focus on classroom management and extra-curricular interests. The practice wasn't as sharp and exacting as that emerging from the leading charter school system.

Teaching methodology

In 2007, Gordon Brown succeeded Tony Blair as Prime Minister. One of first his courses of action was to restructure the DfE. It was to be split into two sections, with Ed Balls leading the Department for Children, Schools and Families and John Denham leading the Department of Innovation, Universities and Skills. However, while the Brown Administration was focusing on structural change the newly appointed shadow education secretary Michael Gove was beginning to speak about classroom practice. In a speech the previous year at Brighton College, he told teachers that a Conservative government would reinstate traditional styles of fact-based lessons. He alleged that generations of children had been let down by so-called 'progressive' education policies which had taught skills and empathy instead of a body of knowledge. He condemned the 'pupil-centred learning' theories which had gained support in the 1960s for 'dethroning' the teacher. He described progressive education as

> 'an approach to education that has been progressive, but in fact is anything but. It privileges temporary relevance over a permanent body of knowledge which should be passed on from generation to generation.... We need to tackle this misplaced ideology wherever it occurs.'

In response, the National Union of Teachers acting general secretary Christine Blower said: 'Gove's attack on child-centred learning is an absurd caricature of reality... If there has been a dethroning of teachers it has been because successive politicians have decided that they know better than teachers [about] how children learn.'

Politicians blamed trendy teaching and teachers blamed interfering politicians, while the students sat at the centre of this ideological debate. I readily admit that the charter schools that I had seen delivered a very narrow curriculum and that they taught to the test but their outcomes were allowing students to break through the glass ceiling to college.

Over many years as a school leader I saw too many newly qualified teachers enter the profession enthused by their tutors in the power of active engagement, collaboration, and differentiation (whatever that means), learning styles, brain gym, etc but lacking a deep understanding of the key building blocks of literacy, oracy and numeracy. University involvement in teacher training is important, and it would be a shame if it disappeared, but I would rather these eager, young novice teachers spent that important year in delving into, and engaging with, the research of what makes effective teaching. Progressive education has the right ideals but, in allowing students to navigate their own way through their learning and setting their own levels of mastery, it can easily lead to institutionalised failure. The problem, for me, with progressive education is that it can trap students within the domain of their own experience if care is not taken. Students from backgrounds which lack aspiration very rarely have a built-in drive to succeed. Their lack of basic knowledge gives them a lower starting point than *their middle-class peers. Their lack of cultural experiences does not give them sufficient background to draw upon when trying to analyse and understand their new learning.*

For me, traditional education puts everyone on a level playing field. It gives everyone the chance to succeed because it puts the acquisition of knowledge, academic rigour, respect and behaviour at the heart of their learning. However, I accept that we do have a responsibility to develop the whole child. As educators we have to find that third way where knowledge, academic rigour and creativity can live in harmony.

Chicago, 2010

In July 2009 Rachel Wolf, an adviser to Michael Gove, set up a registered charity called 'The New Schools Network' with the aim of supporting groups who wanted to set up their own school within the English state system. Wolf started the charity after visiting New York City while working for Gove and observing the work of the city's charter schools.

In May 2010 David Cameron led the Conservative Party to victory in the general election. He immediately appointed Michael Gove to the post of Secretary of State for Education.

In June 2010 Michael Gove set out the government's plans for 'free schools'. In doing so he stated that England had the most stratified, segregated school system in the developed world and that, in order to close the attainment gap, he wanted to learn from what was happening in the US, Sweden, Canada and other countries that had given schools a greater degree of autonomy. Applicants wanting to open a Free school would have to set out their vision, aims and objectives, a curriculum plan and their rationale for setting the school up. They had to supply evidence of demand for their school as well as possible locations for the site.

It was fairly obvious that the Conservative Party had been looking at the possibility of introducing the concept of charter schools in the English education system long before they were elected and had not only researched the best of these schools but had planned the New Schools Network as an arm's length advisory body to help possible applicants. As you can imagine, the fifth tranche of Future Leaders had the possibility of opening up a charter type school at the front of their minds as we touched down at O'Hare Airport that October.

Our schedule was similar to all previous study tours in that we were to visit three charter schools over a period of three days. They were Amandla, Pritzker College Prep and Urban Prep. Amandla was a small charter school that had been founded in 2008 by a group of teachers from the nearby Robeson High School who were disappointed in the standards of the school. Pritzker College Prep had been founded in 2006 and was a member of the Noble Network of Charter Schools and had grown out of Noble Street Charter School. The original school was founded in 1999 through a partnership between Ron Manderschied, President of Nortwestern University Settlement House, and Michael and Tonya Milkie. He network's mission, as stated on their website is to instil in their students, through both love and high expectations, the scholarship, discipline and honour they will need to be college ready and have access to a life rich with options

However, the one that intrigued me most was Urban Prep. It had been founded in 2002 by a group of African-American civic, business, and education leaders, organised by former Hales Franciscan High School President Tim King, who was determined to establish a new all-boys high school in Chicago. At the time, local statistics showed that only one in forty African-American boys in Chicago public schools were graduating from four year university courses and the founders wished to reverse that trend. It was to be the first all-boys charter school in the US.

I had first heard of the school in 2009 when a group of its students was invited to the inauguration of newly elected President Obama. According to the *Chicago Tribune* the manner in which they dressed, spoke and the confidence they had displayed had taken Washington by storm.

Urban Prep was the second school on our visit schedule and I had arranged to meet with senior staff to develop a deeper understanding of the school's culture and curriculum delivery programme. After only a few minutes of conversation I began to realise that there really was something special about Urban Prep and that it went much deeper than their smart uniform.

The mission of Urban Prep chimed with the mission statements of the other charter schools that I had previously visited, in that they were determined to provide a comprehensive, high-quality college preparatory education to young men that results in their graduates succeeding in college. The differences between Urban Prep and the charter schools I had previously visited lay in its values, creed and the breadth of its curriculum.

The school's values were known as the '4 Rs', which encompassed respect, responsibility, ritual and relationships. I immediately pushed back on the use of ritual and relationships as appropriate values needed for college access.

Patiently, it was explained to me that 'ritual' referred to the morning assembly and encompassed aspiration, achievement, pride, respect and hard work among a long list of sub-values. The school firmly believed that creating a strong sense of community would empower students to develop a different mentality to the one they arrived with before enrolment. The purpose of the morning assembly was to start each day with a positive sense of purpose. During the assembly the school deliberately celebrated individual student achievement, and, to further develop individual strength of character, successful students were obliged to stand up in front of their peers to be applauded for their achievements. By making this a daily community activity, students developed a deeper understanding that they were not in it alone and that success is a team game.

The morning assembly began with a chant led by a senior student and repeated, stanza by stanza, by the student body as a whole:

> 'To be early is to be on time
> It is easy to be ordinary
> It takes courage to excel
> Excel we must
> To be on time.'

This was then quickly followed by a small group of pupils playing African drums as a signal that 'community' had begun. On hearing the drums the boys formed up in their 'prides', the name being chosen as a replacement for what we in England would know as tutor groups. The reasoning behind this choice of name was the school's belief that the use of the lion, the school's mascot, as a symbol that could be constantly referred to in encouraging their young students to have the heart, courage and leadership skills of a lion. Throughout the year prides competed with one another, with points awarded for good attendance, high average grade point averages, and inter-school competitions. On the downside, prides lost points for dress infractions, attendance violations, or other disciplinary infractions. The pride with the highest overall point total is awarded the Pride Cup at the annual year-end awards ceremony, known as Tropaia.

As soon as the lines had formed, the assembly was called to order by a member of staff who, using a microphone, shouted 'Good morning Urban Prep!' in a style similar to Robin Williams in 'Good morning Vietnam!' As one, the student body returned the greeting. The teacher then asked 'How are my black, brown, beautiful young men today?' This was a different start to anything I had seen back home. His question was not answered but given a round of applause from the students. The teacher quickly moved on 'Let's check ourselves today'. Students then worked in pairs checking each other's appearance. Looking smart and professional throughout the day was an expectation of the school. After the checking of appearance, the students were urged to 'show each other some love!' This involved the shaking of many hands – teachers included. It was a way of bonding before the formal school day began.

After the bonding ritual, the students returned to their prides and listened to the day's announcements and appreciations. Much was made of the appreciations and many students came to the front to be applauded for exceeding their grade point target or going beyond the '4 Rs' in terms of their attitude but the most coveted award, I was told, was the gold tie. Faculty staff could recommend a student for a gold tie if, in their opinion, the student had been outstanding in the previous week. The gold tie was a symbol of what the school was trying to achieve and was the highest accolade it awarded but, at the end of the week, it had to be returned unblemished so that it could be passed on to another student.

When the awards and notices were finished the students formally recited the Urban Prep Creed before starting class for the day:

We believe.
We are the young men of Urban Prep.
We are college bound.
We are exceptional – not because we say it, but because we work hard at it.
We will not falter in the face of any obstacle placed before us.
We are dedicated, committed and focused.
We never succumb to mediocrity, uncertainty or fear.
We never fail because we never give up.
We make no excuses.

We choose to live honestly, nonviolently and honourably.
We respect ourselves and, in doing so, respect all people.
We have a future for which we are accountable.
We have a responsibility to our families, community and world.
We are our brothers' keepers.
We believe in ourselves.
We believe in each other.
We believe in Urban Prep.
WE BELIEVE!

The creed was a cleverly constructed series of phrases which brought together growth mindset, strong values, aspiration and character development. Like the school songs of the former grammar or independent schools back in England – once learned, never forgotten.

In 1954, at the age of 11, I was lucky enough to win a place at the Liverpool Collegiate, a selective grammar school. In our first week at the school, all new boys had to learn all four verses of the school song in Latin the first verse of which was:

Vivat haec sodalitas, Decus Esmedunae,
Nulli usquam postabenda,
Semper in caelum tollenda,
Magnae virum cunae.

The English translation of the whole song is, for me, quite stimulating.

Long live this fellowship, the order of Esmedune,
Second to none on earth, always raised up to the skies,
A mighty cradle of heroes.

Intellect spurs us on, valour inspires us,
And not forgetting the achievements of our elders,
No less vigorous a generation shall arise.

Now let us remember and celebrate our patrons
Enriched by their generosity, ennobled by their greatness,
let us give them honour.

Long live this fellowship, the order of Esmedune,
Second to none on earth, always raised up to the skies,
A mighty cradle of heroes.

School songs and creeds have long since disappeared from the majority of our English secondary schools. Mine was learned in 1954 and still stays with me to this day. The language level of the translation is very high but the many of the phrases contained within the Urban Prep Creed – growth mindset, strong values, aspiration and character development – are easily identifiable in the Collegiate school song. Many years before these terms became fashionable, some English schools were using the same strategies to build character, cultivate aspiration and high ideals. The urge to modernise education in England may sometimes have thrown the baby out with the bathwater.

My investigations into the design of the Urban Prep curriculum showed that it structured its educational approach through four curricular and extracurricular 'arcs'. These are:

The Academic Arc, which is a rigorous, college-ready curriculum with added focus on reading, writing, and public speaking skills.

The Service Arc, which focuses on deepening the students' sense of responsibility and identification of community needs by completing volunteer programmes within the local community.

The Activity Arc, which focuses on increasing students' confidence, interpersonal skills, and leadership qualities by participating in at least two school-sponsored activities per year. This could include school sports or clubs.

The Professional Arc, which focuses on providing students with valuable experience in a professional environment by requiring them to spend one day a week within such a setting. This serves to reinforce character and leadership development in students, as well as providing them with a means of work experience.

This rigorous approach to developing the whole student was further reinforced through the school's **summer programmes.** During the summer, students are expected to participate in academic, professional, and service programmes throughout Chicago and around the world. Recently, students have attended summer programmes at Oxford and Cambridge universities, as well as elite, home-based institutions such as Northwestern University and Georgetown University.

If this was not enough, all incoming freshmen had to attend a summer induction programme that began in August and ended just before the beginning of the school year.

Of all of the charter schools I had visited since 2006, Urban Prep had, in my opinion, the most rigorous approach and offered many lessons to the schools back home in terms of school culture, community, character building and academic success. It was drilled into every student that the road to success was to not only be accepted for college but to graduate from that college, and that the only hurdle was themselves and their self-belief. Since its foundation in 2006, Urban Prep has become more and more successful at smashing glass ceilings and, at the time of writing, was achieving 100% college access.

It is no wonder that I sat in O'Hare Airport at the end of the visit thinking that, as a school leader, I might have got things a little wrong.

Reflections on Chicago

I accept that much of my writing regarding the study tour to Chicago concentrated on Urban Prep, to the possible detriment of the other two schools. Our visit to Pritzker ably demonstrated Noble Street's determination to change a whole community through the success of its school but Urban Prep had demonstrated a similar vision with a much broader curriculum approach. However, I still had concerns regarding the paucity of the arts curriculum in all of the charter schools I had visited. Urban children do not have the advantages of their more affluent peers in terms of wider arts experience. Each charter school had made a point of ensuring all of their students visited universities so as to enhance aspiration. This, in my opinion, could be augmented by a well-planned cultural enrichment programme with annual visits to museums, art galleries, theatre, and concerts, so as to eliminate any possible cultural deficit that their students may have.

The schools' approach to character building through the use of both rituals and routines in its daily community sessions, as well as the broader academic approach in preparing its students for college readiness, had certainly deepened my thinking regarding the structure of a high aspirations school.

Part 3:
New Beginnings

2010:
The Overnight Flight from Chicago to Manchester

A long time ago I realised that I was one of the few people in the world who did not find flying exciting. I never seemed to get the adrenalin rush that gripped most passengers. Overnight long-haul flights, hunched in a seat watching a film that I was not really interested in, were tedium. However, this flight was going to be different. My mind was racing. I decided that I was not going to take my usual ineffective sleeping tablets and set off to find a stationery shop in O'Hare Airport, as I wanted to buy a writing pad and a couple of spare pens.

By chance, and for the first time in four study tours, I found that I was to be seated away from the main party. Selfishly, I was quite pleased, as I wanted to try and bring together my own learning from the first visit to New Leaders and the three study tours. Since 2006 I had been compiling a mental checklist of the main characteristics that a high performing, aspirational school that was focused on enhancing the social mobility of its students would need to exhibit. It was time to turn the mental checklist it in to a blueprint for a possible free school.

Boarding and taxying to the runway seemed to take an age but, as soon as the seatbelt sign went off, I plunged into my flight bag, took out my newly purchased writing pad and wrote in large letters on the first page:

ASPIRATION HIGH

The academic and cultural blueprint of an 11–18 high school

I had a working title and seven hours before landing to flesh out the blueprint.

Section A: The philosophy
The moral purpose that would drive Aspiration High

There is much evidence that the ability of a child's family to purchase an education at a good independent school can readily enhance that child's social mobility. Seven percent of young people in England gain such an advantage and some fifty percent of places at Oxbridge are awarded to members of this privileged elite. This advantage results in the leading professions being dominated by people educated in the independent sector and it is this domination that restricts entry opportunities to those who are less financially advantaged. This restriction produces a glass ceiling to enhanced social mobility for many state-educated children, particularly those who are being brought up in challenging circumstances. It is easy, as educators in the state system, to be critical of wealth buying enhanced social mobility but such criticism alone will not advance the future prospects our students. If we really want to help them then we must make access to a high quality education the civil rights issue of our generation. If we want to enhance their opportunities and reduce inequality in our society, then the classroom is the best starting point. We have to broaden our mind-sets and accept that educating our young people goes far beyond government targets and Ofsted judgements. It has to become a daily fight for social justice and equality of opportunity for all of our young people. If we are to give them the same advantages as their more advantaged peers then we must lead the fight to produce schools which will match – if not surpass – the quality and breadth of education provided by the best schools in our country including the leading independent schools.

The charter schools that I had visited had convinced me that, given a strong moral purpose, mission driven schools could enhance the life chances of their students and, since 2007, I had been encouraging successive cohorts of Future Leaders in England to open such schools. The study tours had shown them what was possible in America but there were no similar examples in England. It was time to see if such a school would work in England and I was determined that Aspirations High would be that school.

The deep desire to produce a society that offers equality of educational opportunity for all young people, irrespective of their education starting points, family circumstances or postcode, would be the moral purpose that underpinned the daily life of the school. It would be the driving force that energised all who would work in the school. The adults the school employed would need to personally commit themselves to the success of each of their students. They would need to see low educational starting points and financially disadvantaged environments as a challenge to which they must respond rather than use as an excuse for low academic performance. They would need to devise and deliver high quality programmes of education that would address any possible lack of intellectual, social and cultural capital that could hinder their students' educational and social progress. They would have to ensure that these programmes were not only knowledge rich but were explicitly designed to raise the personal aspirations and ambitions of their students, help them develop the strength of character and inner drive to step outside of their comfort zone and understand that failure is a necessary learning experience. If the school could achieve these high ideals then its students would not only fulfil their true potential but be able to compete on equal terms with their more financially and socially advantaged peers. By offering the same high-quality education as the top independent schools, without the burden of fees, Aspirations High would equip its students with the knowledge, skills, strength of character and personal belief to break through any glass ceiling they faced.

An ethical framework

In order to achieve this moral purpose the school would need a strong ethical framework built upon the four cornerstones of beliefs, values, mission and vision. This framework would guide the school in achieving its moral purpose.

The Aspiration High ethical framework

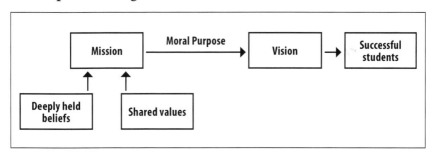

Deeply held beliefs

Deeply held beliefs would be the foundation upon which Aspiration High would be built. Any adult joining the school community would need to firmly believe that:

- a high-quality education is not only an entitlement but a civil right for all young people
- intelligence is malleable and, given the appropriate support and additional time, all young people can succeed at the highest levels

- a knowledge based curriculum, structured by traditional subjects and properly sequenced, is a fundamental entitlement for all students
- aspirations matter and it is the duty of the school to adopt a philosophy of 'no ceilings' in raising the aspirations of its young people
- individual success comes from having the highest expectations of all and accepting no excuses for poor academic performance
- Harnessing the power of knowledge acquisition, character enhancement and leadership development will help our students achieve the social and economic equality needed to compete on a level playing field with their more advantaged peers

Shared values

Aspirations High would need to be as ambitious as the best of the charter schools in having a strong set of values that would be easily memorable. It would have six pillars of character which would not only underpin the daily decisions and actions of the school but would become the lingua-franca of every classroom. These six pillars of character would be known as the ASPIRE Code.

A - aspiration and achievement - through the development of these character traits, we would want our students to develop not only the highest of aspirations but also the drive and determination to achieve those aspirations.

S - self-awareness - by becoming more self-aware, our students would gradually develop a greater understanding of themselves as people, their strengths and, perhaps more importantly, the areas in which they need to develop.

P - professionalism - by taking a 'professional' approach to life in the school it would encourage students to develop 'self-pride' in all that they undertake. Such pride would include being punctual, attending school each and every day, dressing well, presenting their work to the highest professional standards and adopting a professional approach to their behaviour.

I - integrity - the school would help its students to understand that integrity is not just about telling the truth. They would learn that it is about being true to their beliefs and upholding them no matter what situation they were faced with. They would come to understand that integrity is about having pride in all that they do, always working to their true ability and behaving correctly towards other people at all times.

R – **respect** – they would be helped to understand that respect is not simply about being polite, courteous and good mannered. It is about respecting your own ability and working hard to achieve your goals. It is about valuing the differences in others, their background, faith and culture. It is about looking after our planet and its limited resources.

E – **endeavour** – by endeavour, the school would mean working hard to achieve success, being focused on the task in hand, tackling it conscientiously and diligently and having the perseverance, resilience, tenacity and grit to keep going when others start to give up.

A mission-driven school

If the moral purpose of the school was to enhance the social mobility of its students then its mission statement would need to describe how the school would build upon its fundamental beliefs, values and specialism to make that happen. It had to be a statement of intent that would accurately describe its goal.

> *'To harness the power of knowledge acquisition, character enhancement and leadership development to give each of our young people the aspiration, strength of character and self-confidence to fulfil their true potential – no ceilings!'*

The vision for the future of our students

If the mission statement described the methodology that the school would employ to enhance the social mobility of its students then the vision statement would need to describe the outcomes that mission sought to achieve. If enhanced social mobility is our goal then the school would need to recognise that it had to equip each student with a powerful body of knowledge as well as the skills to use this knowledge in as many different situations as possible. To achieve this it would need to work hard in helping its young people develop the necessary study habits to ensure the acquisition of this knowledge as well as the strength of character and self-confidence to push through the glass ceilings they would face on their journey to success. The vision statement would need to describe not only the educational journey the students would follow but where that journey would take them.

> *'To develop in each of our students the academic skills, intellectual habits, qualities of character and leadership traits necessary to succeed at all levels and equip them to become successful citizens in tomorrow's world.'*

The principles that would underpin the curriculum

From this vision statement we can derive the fundamental principles that would underpin the school's curriculum. If the vision is to be achieved then, over time, the curriculum must ensure that each student would:

- increase their intellectual capital by following a broad and balanced academic curriculum built around the EBacc and in line with the leading independent schools. The curriculum would be wedge-shaped in design allowing some subjects to be externally examined in Y10 and no more than 9 subjects to be externally examined in Y11 so as to allow teachers to put depth before breadth and allow sufficient time for mastery in these subjects to be achieved
- develop enhanced aspirations through a planned programme of annual visits to universities
- develop the softer skills of good study habits, positive learning strategies, critical and analytical thinking, personal organisation and time management to help them master their learning. Without mastery of learning, they would not fulfil their potential
- develop the qualities of character needed to maintain sustained attention especially when facing the academic rigour of high cognitive challenge while being thorough and accurate in all that they undertake
- experience a wide range of character building and leadership enhancing experiences to increase their self-confidence while developing the necessary skills to be both a team leader and player. These experiences would include residential outdoor pursuit experiences in Y7 and Y8 as well as all students being entered for the Duke of Edinburgh bronze award in Y9.
- increase their cultural capital through a planned programme of annual visits to art galleries, museums and theatres to gain parity with the cultural capital of their more advantaged peers
- develop the ability to be an effective and, when necessary, persuasive communicator
- develop a strong moral conscience, as well as being socially aware
- develop the self-confidence to succeed irrespective of the completion they faced.

The pedagogical approach that would be needed

The proposed curriculum would be much wider than the conventional secondary school curriculum. The teachers of Aspirations High would need to be able to skillfully interweave knowledge acquisition and character growth in to each of their lessons. This would be achieved through the development of a new pedagogical approach which we would call 'knowledge plus character' teaching.

The essential characteristics of a 'knowledge plus character' lesson would be:

- strong, but not draconian, classroom routines being in place to ensure stress free teaching and liberate learning
- a strong focus on the acquisition and reinforcement of knowledge
- the same 'high expectation' outcomes expected of all students with differentiation being seen as applying the necessary additional support and time that some students may need to achieve these high expectations.
- the best of the charter school's direct instruction approach, without heavy scripting, being used to ensure that newly acquired knowledge is swiftly moved from the short term to the long-term memory
- academic rigour permeating the lesson so that students are continually challenged to think, perform and grow to a level that they were not at previously
- students being continually reminded that failure is a necessary step to long term success
- regular quizzes, tests and assessments informing teachers of the progress of each individual student so that the appropriate support and intervention strategies may be applied when necessary
- strategies continually in place to reinforce literacy, numeracy and oracy
- the ASPIRE Code being continually used as the lingua-franca of the classroom with teachers continually encouraging high aspirations while reinforcing such character strengths as resilience, determination, endeavour and self-confidence through their use of appropriate language

Ethos, climate and culture

Evidence from my visits to the charter schools clearly showed that if young people attended a school where they felt valued, safe and that teachers have their best interests at heart then they committed themselves to working harder, suffered fewer distractions and became more motivated to achieve. This is the ethos that I wanted to create in the school. The school would have to nurture a strong sense of emotional engagement between teachers, parents and students so that they fully understood, and respected, each other's role in maximising the eventual academic success of each of its young people. Values, attitudes and leadership traits could not simply be insisted upon – they had to be continually explained, modelled, reinforced and nurtured by the adults in the school so that permeated the daily life of the school. There had to be strong behavioural norms, not be draconian in nature, that were understood, accepted and followed by the whole community. If students had to line up quietly in lunch queues then so must teachers with nobody pushing to the front! Only by creating such an ethos would students feel not only socially, emotionally and physically safe but prepared to go the extra mile in seeking academic success.

Having established a positive climate the school would need to underpin it through the creation of a 'high expectations' culture which would define the beliefs, values, social norms, rituals, ceremonies and everyday ethos. This culture would be developed through a firm focus on the ASPIRE Code. As with the charter schools, strong visual messages reinforcing the code would greet the students each day as they entered the school. Over every entrance would be the quotation 'We are what we repeatedly do. Excellence, then, is not an act but a habit.' (This is often attributed to Aristotle but is in fact a reworking of one of Aristotle's phrases by Will Durant an American historian and philosopher!). As they walked along the corridors to their classrooms they would be surrounded by inspirational quotations that would focus on each of the values of the Code. They would pass a series of 'You too can be' posters which would illustrate successful career flight paths of leading professionals such as doctors, archi tects, barristers and, of course, teachers so as to raise aspirations. Photographs of leading universities and their specialism would be around every corner that they turned. The classrooms would not be numbered but would be named after a university thus embedding university names in each student's lexicon. Teachers would be asked to display their name and the university they attended on their classroom door so as to encourage aspiration. They would also be asked to display the name of their favourite book to encourage a love of reading in their students. None of these messages were intended to be subliminal. They would be continually referred to by the adults in the school as a fundamental part of its aspiration and character development programme. The intent would be to create an aspirational infection which the students would catch, and for which there would be no cure.

To further support the positive climate and culture the school would develop and maintain a strong network of supportive adults – internally and externally – around each student. The internal support network would be created through the establishment of a 'team around the child' approach which would identify a team of adults who would support and academically challenge each individual student throughout their time at school. . The external network would take longer to establish, as the school would need to develop a network of influential people from the world of higher education, business and commerce, who were supportive of its aims and would be prepared to advise and mentor students on a voluntary basis.

Section B: Philosophy in to practice
Admissions

Aspirations High would not be a selective school. Wherever it was to be situated it would follow local authority admissions guidelines. However, it would operate a pre-entry assessment process so as to determine the individual educational needs of students before entry. Late in the summer term of Year 6, all prospective students would be invited to an assessment morning where they would sit cognitive ability tests so that the school could determine individual learning, support and enrichment plans for all students prior to their September start.

School week

Evidence from the Charter schools showed that a longer school week would be needed if we wished to deliver an enriched curriculum that would result in enhanced outcomes for all of our students. The conventional 25 hours of teaching that the majority of schools have adopted would need to be extended by a further 3 hours with staff being paid above national salary scales to accommodate the change. Over a year this additional time would be equivalent to over 20 additional days of study compared to other state schools. Careful scheduling would allow the school to deliver 6 hours of teaching each day from Monday to Thursday with only 4 hours on a Friday. Such an arrangement would allow Friday afternoons to be dedicated to continuous professional development for the school staff and a longer weekend for the students!

Foundations and senior school

The first five years of the school would be organised in to two separate groupings. The first two years of their secondary education, known as 'foundations', would be dedicated to establishing a solid foundation for senior school. There would be strong and demanding success criteria for the foundations programme which would ensure that, by the end of Y8, all students would be able to read at a level that matched, or surpassed, their chronological age, be able to successfully compute simple mathematical calculations without using their fingers, be able to deliver a prepared speech to an audience of their peers and have acquired sufficient knowledge and problem solving skills to successfully access a three-year GCSE programme starting in Y9.

Senior school would be where GCSE programmes of study would commence. This would not mean taking options at the end of Year 8. A three year-long wedge shaped curriculum, based on the EBacc, would be introduced allowing each student to follow a broad programme of study in Y9 which, over two years, would reduce to 9 subjects at the start of Y11. If appropriate, a limited number of subjects could be examined at GCSE level at the end of Y10 but the school's philosophy would be depth before breadth allowing greater mastery of each subject studied and reducing the overall stress that too many external examinations in Y11 produces.

Delivering the curriculum
The arcs
The curriculum would be delivered through four arcs – the academic arc, the creative arc, the 'character through leadership' arc and the service arc. The academic arc would deliver a knowledge-based curriculum and be taught each morning for four hours on each of the five school days. It would concentrate firmly on the EBacc – English, mathematics, science, history, geography and a modern foreign language. Religious studies and 'character through leadership' would also be accommodated within this arc. Following an EBacc route would give all students equity with the curriculum taught in both grammar and leading independent schools.

The creative arc would be delivered each afternoon from Monday to Thursday. There would be a wide variety of activities on offer such as music, drama, dance, physical education as well as a series of electives allowing students to try specialist individual sports such as fencing, swimming, rowing and jujitsu.

The 'character through leadership' arc would consist of a weekly timetabled lesson and annual residential visits to an outdoor pursuits centre to enhance teamwork and leadership skills. All Y9 students would be expected to follow a programme of activities that would lead to the gaining of the Duke of Edinburgh bronze award. Silver and gold awards could be gained after Y9 but would not be compulsory.

In the service arc time would be set aside each year for students to involve themselves in voluntary public service which, in foundations, could be working in groups to support a local or national charity while senior school would see students becoming involved in personal service projects such as helping in neighbouring primary schools, senior citizens residencies or serving in charity shops.

The learning cycles
If the intent of Aspirations High was to ensure that all of its students reach their full potential, then the way it delivered its curriculum must support this concept. Far too many schools are still locked into three terms of study, interrupted by assessing the progress that their students are making once or twice per year. This approach leaves little room to help correct students' errors,

misconceptions or lack of understanding. Aspirations High would tackle this lack of remediation time through the introduction of five learning cycles that would span the academic year. The first four would be seven weeks in length with the final cycle lasting nine weeks.

The first five weeks of each cycle would be used for the delivery of the knowledge based curriculum, week 6 would become assessment week and week 7 would be 'gap' week where the gaps in student knowledge identified during assessment week could be remediated. Assessments in learning cycles 2, 3, 4 and 5 would be synoptic in that there would always be questions which revisit the learning acquired in previous modules. The additional two weeks in the fifth learning cycle would allow the whole year's learning to be revisited before the final assessment at the end of the year.

Shorter periods of guided learning, objective-led assessment, personalised support, individual remediation and character development would help the school to ensure that each student had 'mastered' their learning. It would be a highly structured approach designed to maximise each student's outcomes.

Programmes of study

Lead practitioners in each subject would prepare the programmes of study for the 24 individual learning cycles that each student would follow from Y7 to the start of external examinations in Y11. The curriculum would be spiral in nature and slowly build, cycle by cycle, continuously revisiting, spacing and interleaving previous learning until sufficient, knowledge and understanding had been acquired and safely stored in the long-term memory by the end of cycle 24 thus allowing students to gain the highest possible grades at GCSE.

Reporting home

At the end of each learning cycle a report would be generated showing each student's progress and attitude to learning, compared to students of similar potential, throughout the cycle. This report would be posted to parents and carers.

Section C: Finding and training the right people

This whole adventure had started in 2006 with my visit to New Leaders. It was there that I first saw how potential mission driven leaders were identified and nurtured. That visit had led to the founding of Future Leaders in England which in turn led to a four year period of visiting successful charter schools. I would need to look no further than the Future Leaders' organisation for the senior appointments. They would all be already aligned with the beliefs, values, mission and vision of the proposed school. They all believed in the need for schools to have a culture of high expectations and no excuses for poor academic performance. They understood that the establishment of strong routines, structures and practices liberated learning in the classroom and, above all, they had visited at least 3 charter schools and seen such practice in action.

As a headteacher, classroom practice had always been my main criteria in appointing new staff. The visit to New York in 2008 had made me realise that finding the right teachers for a mission driven school needed a different set of selection criteria. I would need to find teachers who were not only good classroom practitioners but were mission-driven with a values set that was as closely aligned to those of Aspirations High as possible. When selecting new staff I would reverse the process of looking at classroom practice first and concentrate on allowing the outcomes of a values driven interview to decide who was aligned sufficiently enough with the schools beliefs, values, mission and vision to progress to being observed in the classroom. The observations would not necessarily be looking for the best practitioner on the day but the one who, given appropriate training and support, could progress to being an excellent teacher committed to the school's beliefs and values.

If the school's vision of high outcomes for every student was to be achieved, there would need to be a fierce commitment towards maintaining excellent standards of teaching in every classroom. Allowing schools to close for five days each year for staff training had long outlived its usefulness. By closing early each Friday the school could devote these afternoons to the continuous professional development of all staff. This would be the equivalent of approximately 15 training days each year. To reinforce this commitment all staff would have a coach or mentor who would meet with them on a regular basis. This would allow the school to personalise professional development to individual need.

The induction of new staff, as the school grew in size, would be important. Before starting it would be essential that they fully understood and subscribed to the school's routines, practices and everyday ethos. They would need to attend a pre-starting summer school run by senior staff for which they would be paid.

Section D: Aligning families with our vision

If parents were to be supportive then we would need to follow the charter school example and gain their buy-in before their child was admitted to the school. Rather than have staff visit individual homes we would arrange for the pre-admissions meetings to be held in school during July with a senior member of staff.

The meeting would have three purposes in that it would allow the senior member of staff to:

- check that the school had the right personal information about the prospective student
- ensure that the whole family understood, and agreed with, the schools beliefs, values and expectations
- explain the benefits of the longer school day
- make sure that the family understood the commitment they were making in choosing to send their child to Aspirations High

When it was fully understood, each parent would be asked to sign their section of the commitment pledge and the prospective student would be informed that they would be signing their section at a special welcoming ceremony in September.

At the end of the meeting, the family would be asked to confirm their child's attendance at a Saturday morning assessment where they would sit a series of cognitive ability tests so that the school could personalise its teaching to the child's initial needs upon entry. The senior member of staff would also explain that the first day of term in September would start with a family assembly to formally welcome the family in to the school community and that there would be an informal parents' evening at the end of September so that the school staff could meet with the parents to check that their child had settled in to the school and was coping with its expectations.

In the space of ten weeks, parents would have had three separate meetings with school staff, which would ensure a smooth start for each child and build a firm foundation for a strong parental partnership with the school.

Section E: Inducting Y7 in to the school

Aspirations High was going to be different to neighbouring secondary schools and it would be important that the new students were carefully introduced to its routines, rituals and expectations. I had seen the amount of dedicated time that the charter schools had put in to the induction of new students and decided, as the school grew, all Y7 students would need to start 3 days earlier than the rest of the school. This additional few days would allow school staff time to settle them in and align them with the school's values and expectations. The school would design its own 'character through leadership' programme for these three days so that the students gained a full understanding of the ASPIRE Code and the implications it would have for their daily life in the school. The programme would be deliberately designed to have a degree of fun and enjoyment, as the school would want to ensure an enjoyable transition to secondary education. Formal lessons would not start until day four.

The 3 day character programme would explain each of the school's values using examples of the deeds of famous people. Day one would start by using the conquest of Mount Everest by Hillary and Tenzing in 1953 to illustrate the link between aspiration and achievement. The five camps that the expedition set up to as they climbed the mountain would be used as comparators to the stages in each student's educational journey as they progressed over the next seven years from entering foundations, taking their GCSE's in senior school, taking A-Levels in the sixth form, entering university, graduating and finally accomplishing their mission by successfully entering the world of work. It was important that at the end of day one they would go home with the highest of aspirations and fired up for success!

Days 2 and 3 would draw upon the life and work of Mahatma Gandhi to explain self-awareness; professionalism would draw upon the gruelling training sessions of Jessica Ennis as she planned for the 2012 Olympics; integrity would draw upon the life and dedication of Florence Nightingale; William Wilberforce would be the school's example of respect with his respect for other men in working hard to abolish the slave trade and, finally, endeavour would be modelled by J.K. Rowling in never giving up, despite 12 publisher rejections, in trying to get her first Harry Potter novel published.

Interspersed with these lessons would be a series of well-planned 'fun' exercises to practise the school's routines, with an explanation as to why they were necessary. Teachers would explain that the school thought that it was important that all school sessions started by lining up in the playground and that this was necessary so that classroom teachers could ensure that, by following them, everyone would arrive at the classroom at the same time and that no learning time would be lost through disruption from late arrivals. 'Fun' would be introduced by timing how fast the lines could be formed and using different orders for lining up, such as alphabetical, birth date, size, and so on. During the 'line-up', teachers would emphasise the importance of always looking 'professional' and show how, when in the school lines, each student could help check their neighbour's appearance before leaving the yard for the classroom. Students would be taught the need to walk on the left in corridors on the way to the classroom if overcrowding and log jams were to be prevented. On reaching the classroom, the ritual of shaking the teachers' hand at the classroom door would be demonstrated. It would be emphasised that that this is a sign of respect – one of the school's values – by the teacher for their students and by the students for their teacher. Again, this exercise would be made enjoyable by timing how fast the students could make it happen, so as to save learning time. Teachers would explain that there would not be a free choice as to where to sit but that each class had a seating plan designed to maximise learning and that, as soon as you were in your assigned seat you would need to get out the correct equipment and complete the starter exercise that had been set.

Classroom 'greeters' would be appointed whose role would be to welcome visitors when they knocked at the classroom door, introduce themselves, explain what the class was learning and invite the visitor in to the classroom.

While the teaching of routines would be heavily influenced by the examples I had seen in the many charter schools I had visited, explicitly teaching values in week 1 of Y7 would be, as far as I was aware, unique to secondary schools in England.

As I finished the last paragraph the cabin lights began to flick on. It was 6am and breakfast was about to be served before we touched down in Manchester. The adrenalin rush I had experienced in putting four years of thoughts together had enabled me to ignore tiredness and complete the blueprint for Aspirations High. I hoped that, if it ever materialised, it would be a school that helped its students achieve enhanced academic success and also give them the aspirations and strength of character to break through the glass ceilings to enhanced social mobility. Packing the blueprint carefully into my flight bag, I began to wonder if this was yet another 'new beginning' in my career in education.

Developing Character in the Classroom

The function of education is to teach one to think intensively and to think critically. Intelligence plus character – that is the goal of true education.

Martin Luther King Jr.

The mission of the proposed Aspirations High is 'to develop in each of our students the academic skills, intellectual habits, qualities of character and leadership traits necessary to succeed at all levels and become successful citizens in tomorrow's world'. If the school was to be firm in its intent that all students would succeed at all levels, it would be essential that it worked hard in ensuring that, during their school career, students developed sufficient strength of character to meet the challenges that they would face on their journey to adulthood.

A young person's 'character' is the summation of their values, attitudes and behaviours. Because those qualities are learned, they can also be purposefully taught. Good character doesn't develop automatically, and it's too important to be left to chance if the school's mission was to be successful. Aspirations High would use the phrase 'character education' as an umbrella term for all explicit and implicit educational strategies and activities that the school would employ to help young people develop positive personal character traits. It would not be a subject taught once or twice a week but, instead, an educational approach that, both explicitly and implicitly, would permeate all subjects and become an intrinsic part of the 'invisible' culture of the school.

The school would develop a series of lessons, strategies and practices that would lead to character being caught as well as taught. All teachers would be asked to continually model the behaviours that were implicit in the ASPIRE Code. Well-modelled behaviours would become contagious and pass from the adults to the students who would begin to emulate their behaviours.

The constant application of the ASPIRE Code would help everyone develop a consistent school-wide approach in communicating with students. The teachers would build character by ensuring that all dialogue was firmly rooted in the school's values. The school would use numerous examples when inducting and training its teachers. For example, when a student opens a door for a teacher, the student should be praised for displaying a professional attitude. Failure to open the door would be corrected by pointing out the lack of a professional attitude, thus reinforcing the school's 'professional' value. When a student responds politely to another student in class, the good behaviour would be commended using the 'respect' value with a comment such as 'Sean that was a most respectful way to answer Daisy, well done!' In a reverse situation, the teacher would comment on the 'lack of respect shown in the answer'. Teachers would always be encouraged to comment on the behaviours that the student was displaying and not the person. In commenting on a good answers or a good piece of work the school would ask teachers not to use phrases such as 'That is very clever of you Abdul'. Such approaches imply that students must be 'clever' to produce quality answers. Every teacher in the school had to firmly believe that intelligence is malleable and that the hard work that the student had put into the answer was recognised, rather than the 'cleverness' of the student.

Developing leadership

Alongside character development, the school would develop the leadership strengths of its students. Leading is more about learning specific skills than possessing inherent natural qualities. In this way, being a leader is similar to being an athlete. Certainly, some children are born with attributes that aid in athletics, such as size and quick reflexes, but success in athletics requires thousands of hours of practice to acquire the skills needed for success. There is no substitute for practicing forehands and backhands if you wish to excel at tennis. Ultimately, success in any field is to do with the constant honing of skills through constant practice. By continually offering young people the opportunity to lead, the school would allow them to develop greater personal drive and increase their determination to succeed. Teamwork, risk-taking and developing strategies to positively influence others are all character strengths the school would seek to encourage.

Students would be given a wide range of leadership opportunities. Each day the tutor group lines in the playground would have a different leader to ensure that the group was ready to enter school; tutor groups would have captains, vice-captains and sports leaders with all students given the opportunity to hold at least one of these positions during foundations; each tutor group would elect representatives to the school parliament and the parliament would elect its own cabinet and prime minister who would represent the views of the student body to the school staff.

Y7 and Y8 would attend annual residential leadership experience at the Brathay Leadership Centre in Cumbria and all Y9 students would be entered for the Duke of Edinburgh bronze award in Y9.

2010–2011:
Gathering Support

Having recovered from the overnight flight, I downloaded the 'free school application' form from the DfE website. It was a complex but thorough process and, when completed, would run to over 100 pages. However, three initial actions clearly stood out from the rest of the application, if I was to proceed with it. I would need to form a company which would sponsor the proposed school and find sufficient members and directors to run this company. Deciding on the name for such a company was easy. When Jay Altman and I came together in 2006, we decided that the working mission for Future Leaders was to produce leaders who would establish 'great schools for all children' and that became the company name. Having formed the company, I now needed to find a location for the school and show parental demand in that location by collecting 500 signatures of parents with children in Years 3, 4 and 5 of the local primary schools. The application form further advised that I should inform the local authority of my intent and try to develop a working partnership with them. Having spent the whole of my educational career in the North-West of England I was fully aware of local politician's resistance to academisation – never mind free schools – but decided that contacting a local authority would be my starting point.

I had taught at Brookfield Comprehensive School in Knowsley from 1971 until 1978 and had a very good understanding of the lack of aspiration that permeated the lives of young people in the borough. In 2010 Knowsley, a predominantly white borough, had more than one in five people of working age unemployed and was recognised as being one of the top one hundred areas of deprivation in England. Less than 40% of 16 year-olds were gaining 5'A*-C's compared to the national average of 53% and attendance at secondary school was well below the national average. It seemed the perfect home for Aspirations High. I had known the Director of Children's Services, Damian Allen, for some time and contacted him in the hope of arranging a meeting to discuss my proposal. Damian was very enthusiastic but, despite three meetings, could not garnish the support of the local politicians to the opening of a free school in the borough. Free schools were a 'Tory policy' and not to be touched by a Labour-controlled council. This was the first of many setbacks over the next two years, but I was determined not to give up. There had to be a home for Aspirations High somewhere in the North-West.

Alongside my national and regional duties for Future Leaders, I had agreed to coach three potential school leaders to help reduce the workload of the regional coaches. Shane Ierston, Andrew Reay and David Hayes were all on their residency placement in challenging urban schools. I shared the outline of my proposed school with them and told them of the difficulties I had encountered. Shane had been working at Woolston High, a secondary school in Warrington, before joining Future Leaders. He told me that, despite a lot of parental opposition, the local authority had decided to close the school and that, by 2012, it would be an empty building, but he was still in contact with a local family who had played a prominent part in fighting the closure. It was through Shane's introduction that I first met Colin Scotland.

Colin ran an internet marketing business in Warrington and had played a prominent part in trying to keep Woolston High open. After a brief telephone conversation, he readily agreed to gather a few people together to listen to my proposal for opening a free school. We met on a January evening in 2011 in Colin's office. Present at the meeting was Colin's wife Linda, his sister Claire, and two other sets of parents who had opposed the closure of Woolston High. They listened with enthusiasm to the proposal that I wanted to send to the DfE. Having discussed Aspirations High for almost 90 minutes, I pointed out that the major stumbling block would be collecting the 500 signatures needed before we could submit a proposal. Undaunted they agreed to rise to the challenge and we decided to meet again when they had gained the appropriate number of signatures. I left the meeting thinking that we had possibly taken a small step and that we would probably meet again in March. Seven working days later, Colin rang to inform me that the group had collected 500 hundred signatures and asked what he should do next! In the days following the meeting, Colin and Linda, often under Linda's urging, had positioned themselves outside a different local primary school each day from 7.30am – whatever the weather – and had stayed there until 9am urging parents to sign the petition. To this day, according to the DfE, Colin and Linda still hold the record time for collecting the required number of signatures. Now, I could start to fill in the application form.

I had estimated that it would take some two months to write and submit the bid. Colin and Linda were wary of losing support during this time and urged me to hold a public meeting to meet with the people who had signed the petition. Through their personal contacts, they had already identified a small local church which would allow us to hold a meeting free of charge. They wanted to fix a date and, at their own expense, send out invitations. I readily agreed but was not confident that all 500 hundred people would turn up. When the evening arrived we had to delay the start to find additional space for the enormous number of people who wanted to listen. I decided only to speak for 20 minutes and leave the rest of the meeting for questions. In that 20-minute period, I explained that the proposed school would not be a local authority school, and would be funded directly by the DfE at the same rate of funding per pupil as the local authority received.

I then outlined the four cornerstones of Aspirations High – beliefs, values, mission and vision, the three building blocks of success – intellectual, cultural and social capital that would stand upon the cornerstones as well as the 'character through leadership' programme that would bind everything together. I explained that the fundamental differences between the proposed school and other local schools was that it would start earlier and close later. It would have more lessons each week, homework set every night, a fierce concentration on academic success and well-thought-out strategies which would offer additional support where it was needed so that, given time, every student would reach the highest of standards. I went on to explain that while this support would be a feature of every lesson there might need to be the occasional Saturday morning catch-up session if more intensive support was needed. I told them of the compulsory 'summer school' for students whose attendance dropped below 95% to stop them falling further behind. I described how we would raise aspirations through the development of growth mindsets and regular visits to universities and how we would enrich their cultural experience through regular visits to theatres, museums and art galleries. I explained that there would be strong, but not draconian, behaviour codes that would ensure that there was little, if any, disruption to learning in the classroom.

I could see pictures of disbelief on the faces of some of the young people in the audience but many nods of agreement from their parents. When I stopped and asked for questions a lady in the front row, with a child either side of her, immediately put up her hand and asked 'How soon can you open it?' That was the best start I could have asked for! I fielded question after question for almost an hour and did not hear one word of opposition to the philosophy that would underpin the proposed school. Towards the end of the session, a parent raised his hand and said 'The model you describe sounds like a non-selective grammar school – can that really happen?' That would be the challenge that would face the staff of the proposed school if it opened.

At the end of the meeting we told the parents who were present that we would submit the bid within the next four weeks, with a proposed opening date of September 2012. We had already set up a website for the proposed school and we suggested that any parent with a child in Year 6 follow the Warrington admissions process, but also register their interest on our website.

About two months after submitting the bid, I received a telephone call inviting the 'core group' who had submitted the bid to an interview at the DfE office in London. Colin and I were the core group and with a strange mixture of hope, fear and trepidation we travelled to London. The interview lasted about an hour and concentrated on our ability to deliver what the panel described as an ultra-ambitious vision. We must have been convincing in our response because, towards the end of 2011, I received another telephone call telling me that the proposal had been agreed and Aspirations High could become a reality.

2011–2012:
The Rocky Road to Opening

The next nine months were to become possibly the most challenging time in my educational career. Soon after the telephone call, Colin and I met with Davinder Girn and Michelle Turner of the DfE and Mike Foy of the Education Funding Agency at the DfE offices in Runcorn. These three people were to become our guardian angels in guiding us towards the successful opening of the free school. At that first meeting they gave us four pieces of sound advice, based on their experience of establishing the first wave of free schools. They urged us to try to develop a cordial relationship with the local authority, secure an intake of students for September 2012, start recruiting teachers and think about changing the name of the school to something more august.

The DfE had already written to Warrington local authority to inform them of its decision to open a free school in Woolston and, immediately after our meeting, I followed up this letter with a request to meet the Director of Children's Services in the hope of establishing a 'cordial relationship'. Kath O'Dwyer was Director of Children's Services at the time and she agreed to meet Colin and myself to discuss the DfE's letter. While the meeting was cordial, it was obvious that the authority was not happy with the idea of a free school opening in Warrington. When we asked about the possibility of moving into Woolston High after it closed in August 2012, Kath said that it was unlikely to happen but agreed that we could have an 'escorted' tour of the building. We left the meeting with a sense of unease. It had not been unpleasant but we had been unable to establish the relationship we needed for a smooth opening.

On the day of our visit, the head of the school gave us a warm welcome and we were shown into an office where Hilary Smith, the local authority's representative, was waiting for us. Within minutes of our arrival a representative of the EFA arrived to join the tour, in order that he could prepare a report on the building's suitability for the proposed free school. However, just as the tour was about to commence, Kath O'Dwyer walked through the door and announced that the authority had decided to close Green Lane and Foxwood Special schools and bring them together on the Woolston High campus and that, as the site would no longer be available, the tour was cancelled. When I politely asked why we had not been told of this at our previous meeting, I was informed that the decision had only just been taken. It was becoming fairly obvious that we would have to become very resilient and determined if we were to successfully open a free school in Warrington. When we informed Michelle Turner about what happened, she advised us to press on and leave her to make further contact with the local authority.

Despite this setback we decided to call a meeting of all parents who had registered their desire for their Year 6 child to transfer to the free school in September. Applications from Year 6 for secondary education in Warrington had closed some time ago and all of the parents readily admitted that they had followed our advice and chosen a Warrington school as their 'school of choice' for their child. Despite this, it was a positive meeting and they agreed that, if we could find a building, they would stay with us.

The summer resignation date for experienced teachers was fast approaching. We needed to recruit a core staff despite not having an intake or a school building. There was still teacher opposition to free schools and, despite a national advert, only two people applied for the post of founding principal. One of the applicants was Shane Ierston, who I had coached over the previous 12 months for Future Leaders. There was obviously going to be a conflict of interest and, to ensure impartiality, it was agreed that DfE representatives would sit on the panel and that I would adopt observer status, with no voting rights. Shane's commitment to the project came through loud and clear and, as such, he was duly appointed. Following other national adverts and word-of-mouth searches, Andrew Reay was appointed deputy principal and teacher of both geography and P.E., Toni Coase was appointed to teach mathematics, Katie Sharp was appointed to teach English and Nicola Burrows, for two days a week, to teach history. We would need to beg, steal or borrow additional part-time expertise to bring the costs as near as possible to the income generated by such a small cohort.

Finding an alternative building to Woolston High School in which to open was proving a difficulty. Michelle and Pavinder from the DfE took over all meetings with the local authority so as to establish a more cordial relationship, while Mike Foy searched for a site. The DfE had the power to force the authority to hand over Woolston High but were understandably reluctant. It was only the second year of the free school programme and they did not want to get into a legal battle, especially when the council's case was that they were improving the education facilities for children with special needs. It was at this point that Mike Foy came to the rescue. He had carried out a search of every commercial building in the area, as well as determining the spare capacity of local schools, to see if he could find us a temporary home for our proposed school. As a result of this search he discovered that Bruche Primary School in the Padgate area of Warrington had an almost empty building on their campus. It was formally an infants' school but falling numbers had led to the infants relocating to the adjoining building which housed the rest of the primary school students. To help the primary school with the running costs of the empty infants' building the council had leased part of it to a teacher training company but a small school hall, five classrooms with a set of infant-sized toilets in each and an office remained vacant. It was very small and did not have either adult toilet facilities or a kitchen to cook school lunches, but it would house two Year 7 classes on a temporary basis. Eventually, after much legal wrangling, the council agreed to lease the site to the new school on a temporary basis.

However, before a funding agreement could be signed we had to work out an agreement with the local authority regarding the establishment of a permanent home for the school. Surprisingly, the council agreed that we could apply for planning permission to build a new school on a local playing field. Both parties knew that such an application would bring Sport England into the dispute and that we would possibly face opposition regarding the loss of green space. Nonetheless, the DfE were prepared to accept this challenge and the funding agreement was drawn up and signed. Albeit small in area, Warrington was about to see the opening of its first free school. Unfortunately, the final agreement was not reached until mid-June 2012. This gave us with about ten weeks to finalise the intake of students for the new academic year, and find a contractor to refurbish the school, install adult toilets and get it ready to open.

While all of this was happening we turned our attention to the name of the proposed school. Aspirations High had always been a working title and, as suggested, we tried to think of something more august that would suggest high standards and emulate the schools in the independent sector. As a head in Manchester, I had followed the school's debating team each year as they challenged local independent schools for an annual trophy. Wherever I went I seemed to be in a King's School. In the local heats, the school was often drawn against King's School Chester or King's School Macclesfield. Winning the local heats pitched you against independent schools in a wider area and, invariably, there was another King's School somewhere. We decided to call the school King's and immediately ran into trouble. You had to be named by Royal Charter to assume the King's name. We wrote to Buckingham Palace who referred us to the Cabinet Office in Downing Street. After several rounds of correspondence, it was agreed that we could call it King's if we followed it with a descriptor to define the school's specialism. It was Andrew Reay who suggested that as our specialism would be 'character through leadership' we should consider calling the school King's Leadership Academy. It was distinctive, it expressed what we wanted to achieve and it had a nice ring to it. We had a name, now we needed an intake.

The time it had taken to secure a site had had an adverse effect on the number of parents who had agreed to stay with us, but we were confident that at least 39 new students would turn up in September. To further encourage them to sign up we managed to find a uniform supplier, School Colours, who were prepared to help us design and make a uniform – despite the low numbers – and a local firm, Parker Design, to produce a badge that reflected the new name. Once again, the local church came to our rescue by allowing us to have an evening where sample blazers and jumpers could be tried on and ordered. Once the parents had committed to purchasing the uniform we knew our first intake was secure.

With wizard like efficiency Mike Foy managed to find a building firm who were confident that they could refurbish the building within eight weeks. They were on site within two weeks and set about painting walls and blocking off the infants' toilets. A set of portable toilets were brought in by crane and lifted over the building to be installed on the small playground, furniture was ordered and a kitchen much smaller than you would find in an average house was fitted.

We wanted to give the new school a corporate brand and turned, once again, to Parker Design to ensure that all signage had a corporate image. The badge they had designed had a rampant lion either side of a shield and they suggested that we incorporate the lion in all of our signage. Scouring the internet, we managed to find concrete lions, later to be called Aristotle and Archimedes, which were ordered to stand outside the front entrance.

By August, our attention had turned to finding a meal supplier. Being on the same campus as Bruche Primary School, we approached the local authority to see if the cooks in the primary school could prepare the meals for us. Unfortunately, the price they quoted was prohibitive. Using local contacts we found a small one-person organisation who catered for dinner parties and receptions. We tried to ring her but were told by her husband that she was in France on holiday with their children. However, he was intrigued by our request and promised to contact her. She rang the next day and we managed to come to an agreement that she would deliver cooked meals to the school for at least the first two months of the autumn term. Having arranged the catering, we needed to buy 50 sets of knives, forks, spoons, plates, pudding dishes and drinking glasses. A shopping spree to IKEA was quickly organised.

Ordering stationery was to prove to be another brick wall. The major stationery firms that dealt with schools wanted credit checks and purchasing histories, which we couldn't supply. Unabashed, we went on yet another shopping spree but this time to Poundland where we bought enough pens, pencils, rulers, exercise books, staple guns and glue sticks to see us through until half term.

The builders handed the refurbished building over to our team just two days before the term was due to start. The two training days we had planned were immediately cancelled and the team set about unpacking furniture, arranging classrooms, producing wall displays to cover the pristine white walls that surrounded us and formally naming each classroom after the university that its teacher had attended. We managed to find some part-time staff just before opening. We found a retired mathematics teacher who agreed to act as both receptionist and cover assistant if required. Shane managed to negotiate an agreement with his former school to have two language teachers for a total of six periods per week. We had found enough professional sports coaches to put together an elite sports programme of fencing, rowing and jujitsu while the Liverpool Institute of Performing Arts provided our musicians and drama instructors. We would be able to offer a broad curriculum that was as close to being balanced as we could manage. I would become an unpaid public speaking teacher and, for the first few weeks, act as kitchen assistant serving meals and washing dishes until we could afford a lunchtime assistant.

It had been a hectic and challenging summer but on Wednesday 5th of September 2012 we opened the school doors to admit our first free school intake of 39 students. The base camp for our assault on the glass ceilings that restricted the enhanced social mobility of too many young people had been established.

Reflections on Opening a Free School

Free schools are independent state schools. They can be set up by charities, groups of teachers, existing schools or parents if they can prove that they are needed and wanted by a local community. Local needs can be defined as any, or all, of the following.

- *A shortage of school places in a particular area.*
- *Limited access to quality education in their area.*
- *Raising educational standards, or offering a different choice, in a community.*
- *Providing unique support for students with particular educational needs.*
- *Providing quality education in deprived areas.*

To apply to set up a free school, you must complete the application form supplied by the DfE. It is not an easy process and you will need to bring together a committed core team, with a range of skills, who are willing to work on a voluntary basis.

There are three key areas that you will need to consider before applying.

1. *Showing that there is a clear demand for the type of school you are proposing in your area.*

2. *Constructing a clear vision for the proposed school that encompasses what you want it to achieve. This vision will act as the cornerstone in guiding all decisions you will make about the school as you move through the application process.*

3. *Your ability to bring together a group of volunteers who have the relevant skills to put together a strong proposal.*

It usually takes three to six months for the team to write and submit the bid. The DfE will take up to six months to assess your bid. You will be invited to an interview if they think your bid is of the correct quality and that your team has the right expertise to bring the project to fruition. If your bid is approved you will enter the 'pre-opening phase' during which you will work with the EFA to find a site, recruit the necessary staff and market your new school. Most free schools open at the start of the academic year in September and you should build this into your planning timeline.

It is not meant to be an easy task but there can be an immense feeling of satisfaction in bringing a project to fruition.

2012–14:
The Early Years

The first term in the free school started well. The team had met many times during the summer and had fully immersed themselves in understanding the cultural blueprint that would underpin the daily life of the newly named King's Leadership Academy. We worked together to write a three-day, student-centred 'introduction' programme aligned to the beliefs and values of the new school, which included games and competitions to embed the routines that needed to be established if long-term success was to be achieved.

At 8.30am on the first Wednesday in September, the free school opened with a family assembly during which Shane Ierston, as principal, outlined our vision for a successful secondary education and the beliefs and values that would underpin that education. He thanked the parents for having the faith to stay with us and promised them that each and every child would fulfil their potential and become 'a successful citizen in tomorrow's world'.

During those first three days the students were taught how to make a firm handshake while making full eye contact and why lining up in quiet lines at the end of breaks and lunchtimes could save endless learning minutes on their journey to academic success. They used the planning behind the successful ascent of Mount Everest in 1953 as an exemplar for planning their own future. They learned the names of the principal universities in the region, as well as the country as a whole, and planned their career 'flight path' so that they could aspire to one day land their dream job. Using a mixture of historical and present day figures, they began to understand the benefits of having a strong values code and this was all before the formal curriculum was introduced. On the Friday afternoon of that first week, parents were invited in to witness what has now become the academy's induction ritual – the tie ceremony. The tie ceremony represents the formal admission of each student to the academy. Part of the students' induction programme involved revisiting the 'student commitment contract' and, during the ceremony, they would come to the front of the hall to sign their contract and formally receive their school tie as a recognition of their admission to the academy.

On that first Friday, the small infants' hall was completely full of expectant parents wondering why they were back in the school so soon. Before the ceremony started, Andrew Reay explained the purpose behind the ceremony and, to the background of the triumphal march from Verdi's Aida, each student came to the front and signed their contract of commitment, as well as a pledge to follow the ASPIRE Code, before receiving their King's tie. The end of the ceremony was met with tumultuous applause from the parents and many warm compliments on what we were setting out to achieve. The academy's first ritual had been successfully implemented and it is as successful each new school year as it was on that heady afternoon. Afterwards, the staff were tired after a strenuous first three days but were eagerly looking forward to the introduction of the formal curriculum on the following Monday morning.

After much discussion during the months before opening, the team decided that the school would go, as far as possible, paperless. This meant a heavy investment in iPads, but we had calculated that we would cover this investment in reduced photocopying costs and, where possible, by using fewer textbooks. The idea was that we would enter the flipped learning era by teachers emailing each student the notes and PowerPoints that were to be used in the next day's lessons, so as to save learning time.

A further initiative was to be the introduction of silent reading each morning to enhance reading ages and encourage a love of reading. Students could bring in their own book, download a daily young people's newspaper we had decided to subscribe to, or access one of the classics online.

It was agreed that we should set out to achieve the highest of standards in each lesson by pitching our expectations high and scaffolding down to provide additional support and time where it was needed most. This was quite challenging in the early days. We might have had a comparatively small cohort but the initial spread of abilities was quite wide and, if every student was to be successful, we needed to keep in-school variation to a minimum. This was helped by the introduction of the learning cycles. Every sixth week we would assess progress during the learning cycle, forensically analyse the assessments and use week seven to correct any misunderstandings or misconceptions.

Placing the academic arc in the morning session and the creative arc in the afternoon proved to be an excellent idea. Not having a sports hall or gymnasium, we had to become imaginative in our thinking as to the creative offering. We found part-time expertise in both art and music but had to consider alternative sports to the normal range of team games. Fencing, jujitsu, rowing and dance were all introduced in the academy's first year and still play a prominent role today.

We placed great emphasis on public speaking throughout the first year. Our intent was to give each student both the confidence to speak well in public and the ability to construct a persuasive argument when debating in class.

Another feature was the introduction of family dining from day one. This allowed teachers and students to get to know each other outside of the classroom environment. We would use this time to encourage the development of both conversation skills and dining table etiquette.

The first few weeks went well. Lessons were of the highest quality, line-ups were exemplary and, above all, the lunches from the outside caterer arrived on time. The only grumbles were from me as I set out the dining room and washed the lunch dishes each day. We needed to buy a dishwasher and hire a lunchtime assistant. The EFA took pity on me and, by half term, we had further assistance so I was eventually able to hang up my rubber gloves!

Andrew and Shane introduced a wide range of leadership roles into the school. Alongside the usual roles of form, house and sport captains, they introduced the concept of class greeters who would meet the growing number of visitors at the classroom door and outline the learning that was taking place in the lesson. Environmental leaders were introduced to look after the internal and external parts of the school environment each break and lunchtime and a school parliament, whose members would be voted into office each year, was set up.

Prior to opening, Andrew had introduced me to Godfrey Owen, the CEO of the Brathay Trust. Brathay is an outdoor pursuits centre based in Ambleside in Cumbria. Its mission is 'to improve the life chances of children, young people and families by inspiring them to engage positively in their communities'. The trust seemed an excellent partner through which we could deliver the outdoor pursuits part of our 'character through leadership' programme and we quickly agreed that all of our students would attend Brathay for at least one residential experience each year.

At the end of September, our new Year 7s first experienced the delights and challenges of Brathay! For two days, working in teams and alternating leaders for each activity, the students walked up Cumbrian fells, crossed fast flowing streams, rowed to the centre of a lake and back and attempted the Brathay assault course. Each activity not only gave them a better understanding of teamwork and what it meant to lead but encouraged them – with the support of their team – to step outside of their comfort zone and, in doing so, gain increased confidence.

Aspirations were boosted through trips to a local university and a residential trip to Sidney Sussex College in Cambridge. Cultural capital was developed through visits to at least one theatre, museum and art gallery, all in their first year.

Shane Ierston is an excellent leader and team builder. He worked relentlessly at bringing the full-time, part-time and visiting staff together as one team determined to support the academy's mission of harnessing the power of knowledge acquisition, character enhancement and leadership development to give each of their young students the aspiration and strength of character to fulfil their true potential. Andrew Reay, drawing upon his military experience, became the academy's expert on developing character through leadership and strategic planning for our second academic year, while Shane concentrated on coaching the staff to produce the highest of expectations in their classrooms. Together they were to produce a powerful partnership.

My role as conductor to this small orchestra was drawing to a close, as Shane and Andrew took over the reins in bringing the dream to its next stage. I now had to look at designing the new school and applying for planning permission.

Working with the EFA, we started planning for the permanent site. The proposed building would be 6,800 square meters in area and cater for 840 secondary and sixth form students with 50 classrooms, a sports hall, a multi-use games area and pitch, gym, fitness studio, double height colonnade and feature entrance. Sustainability features would be incorporated throughout the design including a natural ventilation system with louvres integrated at the top of the windows. Swales would also be created in the corners of the site to store and collect surface water run-off which would then be used as ecological garden spaces. Having drawn up the plans the EFA worked hard with Sport England and Warrington's planning department to remove all possible obstacles and gain their approval before the plan was submitted to the planning committee. At the request of Sport England, compromises in the design were willingly made to increase the community use of the building so as to compensate for the loss of one corner of the playing field on which the proposed school was to be built.

The planning committee meeting was well attended, mostly by supporters of the proposed new school building. Sadly and somewhat predictably, against the recommendation of the council's own planning officer, permission was refused. Despite this further setback we were determined not to give up. There was little alternative but to appeal to the Secretary of State, Eric Pickles. Early in 2014, after considerable deliberation, he announced that he disagreed with the decision of the planning committee and we were given the all-clear to start building. Before anyone else changed their mind, the EFA pressed the start button and building work commenced. The opening date was agreed as September 2015 – at last, another hurdle had been cleared.

The building was quick to take shape and by February 2015 two floors and the roof were almost completed when we discovered, by accident, that the builders were having cash flow problems. In March 2015 they went into liquidation and all building work stopped. Fortunately the EFA acted incredibly promptly in sealing down the site and securing Conlon Construction as the new building firm. There would obviously be a delay in opening but the new builders were confident that they could hand it over by June 2016.

The original application had been submitted in 2011. June 2016 would mark the end of a five-year journey and the start of our mission to show that the glass ceilings of social mobility could be broken.

Reflections on Building a New School

In March 2014, the EFA published new guidelines for school design so as to allow as many schools as possible to benefit from the limited funds available. These guidelines advocated a 'no frills' approach without compromising teaching or school organisation. A funding-led design prevented the huge costs incurred in the 'Building Schools for the Future' project where architects ran wild with curved corridors, glazed roofing and incredible atriums that became difficult to clean.

The new funding formula suggested that the gross area of a secondary school should be calculated by the formula:

$1050m^2$ (+ $350m^2$ if there is a sixth form) + $6.3m^2$/pupil place for 11- to 16-year-olds + $7m^2$/pupil place for post-16s.

For primary schools the new formula is:

$350m^2$ + $4.1m^2$/pupil place.

This has started to limit the previous financial excesses of imaginative architects who will now start their initial meeting with you by asking how many students your new building will need to accommodate and then telling you how many classrooms your design will have. I would recommend that, at this point, you gather the strength to stop the conversation and ask if you can start again, but with your vision for how you want your school to work rather than being told what you will be getting. You will not be allowed to move outside of the guidelines but your architect will have a better idea of what you want.

To determine your vision you need to adopt a 'design-thinking' approach to the daily life of the school.

- *What will your teachers need in each classroom? Will they need three whiteboards at the front of the classroom with one main working space, a separate smaller board for displaying the lesson objectives and a third small board for such things as recording rewards and infractions?*

- *Will their classrooms need projection points that connect readily with their iPads to bring up lesson notes or videos?*

- *Is there sufficient storage space to accommodate the storage of text and exercise books as well as specialist equipment?*

- *How will the corridors work during transitions? Will the corridors be wide enough to manage the flow?*

- *How will lunchtime be managed? Will the space available need 'sittings' to be introduced? Can it accommodate family dining?*

- *Where will the students play during break and lunchtimes and how will they re-enter the building?*

- *How will your sports hall work? What team games will it accommodate?*

- *How will natural light be allowed into the building?*

These are just a few of the many questions you need to ask yourself before that first meeting with the architects. By using a 'design-thinking' approach you can involve staff and students in constructing your vision. It will still have to be accommodated within the new funding-led guidelines but it will allow you to have an educational input into the design.

2014–15:
The Hawthorne's

In March 2014, some three weeks before the builders in Warrington went into liquidation, I received a telephone call from the DfE asking if I had the capacity to help The Hawthorne's Free School in Bootle which, 18 months after opening, had been judged by Ofsted to be inadequate and a cause for concern.

The school, which had opened at the same time as King's Leadership Academy in Warrington, was the result of a successful bid from a group of dedicated teachers from St. George of England High and St. Wilfred's High in Bootle, South Sefton. Both schools were subject to closure by the local authority and steps were already in place to transfer their students to other neighbouring schools. However, the teachers in the two schools knew their students well and were afraid that a transfer to another school would have an adverse effect on their GCSE outcomes. Despite falling birth rates and an aspirational drift by many 11-year-olds to the leafier parts of the borough, they were determined to preserve a secondary school in the area for their students by successfully submitting a free school bid.

At the time of the Ofsted inspection there were 358 students on the roll of the free school, with one in every two being in receipt of pupil premium funding compared to the national average of 28.7%. One in five of its students had been identified as having special educational needs at the school action stage, which was twice the national average, and despite only being open for 18 months, its roll was already falling.

I knew Bootle well having grown up some three miles from the school. It was classified as being one of the most 'socio-economically deprived' areas in

England. The wards served by the school were in the bottom 5% for economic deprivation, the bottom 2% for employment and the bottom 8% for crime. Since 2006, I had been training Future Leaders' participants to lead schools with similar socio-economic profiles and King's Warrington was successfully turning the training rhetoric into practice albeit in not such a challenging area as Bootle. Thinking that the Warrington project was on track, I readily agreed to help.

The Ofsted inspection had revealed weaknesses in the quality of teaching. The inspectors had identified some good teaching but reported that it was not consistent across the school. Opportunities to correct and enhance literacy and numeracy skills were being missed in several subject areas and there was inconsistency in the challenge offered to the more able students. An examination of the school's finances had shown that it was difficult to link the spending of the pupil premium grant to the strategies being used to close achievement gaps.

Inspectors also found inconsistencies in the use of both data collection and input, making it difficult to track student progress and interrogate the overall performance of the school. A deeper analysis of the data the school had on hand revealed that the performance between differing groups was increasing despite the school's intervention strategies. During their meeting with the school governors, the inspectors gained the view that the data that governors were presented with was too complex and lacked a clear message. It was a bit of a mess but I had seen worse.

I did not want to be parachuted in as a 'turnaround expert'. I had seen such practices fail before. If the turnaround process was to be successful then the governors and senior leaders needed to be partners in the recovery journey and my role would be to act as a catalyst for change. I agreed to meet a group of governors and, after a 20-minute conversation about my education philosophy, they decided that they wanted my help, but they also wanted to retain the 'progressive nature' of their school. Their preferred brief was for me to spend two days each week working with the existing principal to bring the school out of special measures.

Ofsted inspections are a snapshot in time of the journey a school is making. Inspectors are usually efficient at identifying weaknesses in performance but they rarely have time to find the root cause of the problem. The spring break was only two weeks away and I wanted to spend that time digging deeper into the schools practices and procedures to find where the real problems lay.

An analysis of attendance trends showed that there was a wide variation in the attendance of pupil premium and non-pupil premium students and an unacceptable number of persistent absentees. Further investigation showed that many of the persistent absentees were mid-year entries, usually from the council's Fair Access scheme, who arrived with an existing history of non-attendance. The school had readily admitted these students but had failed to make any of them subject to a personal support plan or regular monitoring of their attendance. While there seemed to be a lot of individual home visits to encourage attendance there was no evidence of an ongoing analysis of trends and variations. Far too many students were taking occasional days off school and there was little accountability in terms of explaining their absence when they returned. Rewards to encourage regular attendance had not been considered.

The systems for tracking student progress were inadequate, with much data missing. A fresh start would be needed.

A thorough examination of the school's finances showed that the pupil premium grant which, given the high numbers of pupils in receipt of the grant was not inconsiderable, was not ring-fenced and difficult to track. Without ring-fencing it was not possible to see if the spending of the funds was effective in narrowing the achievement gap.

Lesson visits had shown me that there was a lot of good practice around the school. I identified a strong nucleus of dedicated teachers who, behind their closed classroom doors, were working tirelessly in seeking success for their students. However, a small but significant number of teachers were not performing at the same high level as their colleagues. In their lessons, opportunities for reinforcing access skills were not being identified, they were 'teaching to the middle' and the more able students were certainly not being stretched. The problem seemed to be the absence of a clear, school-wide vision for student development or, if there was, it was hard to identify and certainly not being clearly communicated to the students themselves.

In the first year of the school a group of staff had worked hard at producing a set of values that would guide the daily life of the school. They had proposed achievement, community and excellence (ACE) as their set of values. Unfortunately, despite their efforts, these values had not been adopted on a school-wide basis, resulting in a lack of shared values and expectations. The school had many hidden strengths but needed a stronger sense of agreed purpose as to what it was trying to achieve and a good set of values to drive that sense of purpose forward.

If the turnaround was to be successful, the starting point had to be working with the leadership team in accepting the findings of the Ofsted report and stopping the 'blame culture' that had developed since its publication. The inspection had taken place in the first week of February and, some eight weeks later, there was no indication of a detailed recovery plan being produced.

Two days before the spring break I met with the head to discuss what I thought needed to happen. During the course of the discussion it became clear that the writing of a recovery plan had not been discussed at senior team meetings. Ofsted would be back within three months and we agreed that this had to be our first priority. The plan had to be wider than the areas for improvement identified during the inspection. It had to give the school a new sense of direction and purpose. It had to promote the highest of expectations and tolerate no excuses for poor academic performance.

Within two weeks of the start of the summer term we had a recovery plan. Each of the key priorities from the previous inspection was given a separate section, with a detailed set of actions in order to achieve the well-defined targets. Ambitious timescales were set, reflecting the team's desire to come out of special measures as quickly as possible.

The plan necessitated a thorough overhaul of attendance strategies. Non-teaching pastoral staff were reorganised to ensure rigorous monitoring of attendance. All persistent absentees were written to and warned of the legal consequences of not returning to school. Several did return and attendance support plans were immediately put in to place. Cutting persistent absence was going to need a constant long-term focus. An attendance panel was set up to work with individual students in stopping the practice of taking occasional days off. A rewards system was introduced for good attendance and punctuality and, by half term, an increase in regular attendance could be identified.

Having witnessed the success of the learning cycles in Warrington, the leadership team drew up plans to implement the same system for the next academic year so that regular progress data could be analysed and necessary interventions planned. A strategy that mirrored King's Leadership Academy was introduced to monitor students' achievement at the end of each learning cycle. This would allow senior and middle leaders, as well as class teachers, to keep a close eye on how well individuals and groups of students were doing, not only in their own subject but across a range of comparable subjects. Senior leaders would now be able to identify students who were off target and produce suitable intervention strategies.

Little could be done regarding the present spending of pupil premium funding but the plan specified the introduction of ring-fenced funding from the start of the next financial year and strategies were produced to measure the effectiveness of the spending in terms of closing achievement gaps.

A member of the senior team was given the freedom to rejuvenate the school's approaches to triangulating lesson observations, work scrutinies and the quality of teacher feedback. This was beginning to address the serious weaknesses in teaching that had been identified in the February inspection.

A short- and long-term plan for improving the visible ethos of the school was put in place. A long-term painting schedule had been produced and a local firm was employed to carry this out. Aspirational posters were displayed in each corridor. Large television screens, placed at strategic points in the school, ran programmes on loop encouraging high expectations. The school was starting to develop a distinct rhythm to its daily routines, morale was rising and enthusiasm returning. A positive school climate was being established, as well as an academy-wide culture of high expectations.

In July, Ofsted returned. The section 8 report was very positive about the changes that the school had made but contained the following comment:

> 'The responsibility for driving forward the school's improvement agenda is heavily invested in the interim executive principal, who is working hard to make up for the deficit in senior leadership capacity.'

September saw the school looking for an interim principal.

Michael Taylor was a graduate from the second cohort of Future Leaders. He was a mature entrant to the profession and had shown considerable leadership ability during training. I had worked with him for two terms on a turnaround project and knew his strengths well. Since graduating from Future Leaders he had developed a growing reputation regarding his ability to help schools move out of category. I rang Michael to check on his availability, despite him living in Hertfordshire. He was still a deputy headteacher and had just assisted his present head in helping her to move her school out of special measures. Fortunately, he had a verbal agreement with her that she would release him early if the chance of a headship came up and, when he explained the situation to her, she agreed to waive notice. Michael did not want to leave Hertfordshire on a permanent basis but readily agreed to commute to Bootle on a weekly basis.

It did not take long for the school's leadership team to recognise Michael's strengths. His strategic planning and organisational capabilities not only added great strength to the senior team but increased their motivation to bring the school out of category as soon as possible. New lines of accountability were established and existing practices were made even tighter. The second monitoring visit in November, just two months after Michael had been appointed, recognised the great strides the school had made. By the third visit in March 2015, we were beginning to feel confident that the school was almost ready to come out of category. In June, the section 8 became a full inspection and the school was taken out of category. We had applied the same educational blueprint as we had used in the 'start-up' free school in Warrington and it had been successful in a much more challenging area!

2015–16:
A Further Challenge

In 2012, Shorefields Community School in Toxteth, Liverpool successfully applied for academy status and became a member of the University of Chester Academies Trust (UCAT). It had its first Ofsted inspection as an academy in March 2014 and had been judged to have serious weaknesses.

At the time of the inspection, it was smaller than the average secondary school and had significantly more boys than girls. Approximately 50% of its students were of white British heritage with the remaining students coming from a diverse range of minority ethnic groups. 85% of students were supported by pupil premium funding and some 50% percent spoke English as an additional language. The inspection had judged leadership, governance, and quality of teaching as inadequate. The behaviour and safety of pupils was judged to be requiring improvement.

By the time of the first monitoring visit, just three months later, UCAT had appointed a new senior leadership team to the academy. Over the next 12 months many changes were made but, unfortunately, they were taking longer than expected to bring about an improvement in the academy's performance.

In May 2015, the DfE decided to change the academy's sponsor, citing an ongoing concern regarding UCAT's sponsorship, consistently low GCSE outcomes and the lack of progress made by the interim leadership team. Paul Smith, who was Regional Commissioner for Lancashire and West Yorkshire at the time, tried to find a new sponsor, without success. When UCAT suggested closing the school instead of re-brokering, recognising the success of both King's Leadership Academy and The Hawthorne's, Paul asked if I would consider forming a multi-academy trust with myself as CEO to bring all three schools together under the one umbrella. Although the EFA had managed to secure new builders for King's Warrington, and The Hawthorne's looked as though it would soon come out of category, I was quite hesitant. It was a nice vote of confidence in what the team was achieving but I was unsure that we had the capacity to take on a third challenge so soon. I asked for extended time to undertake due diligence before making a decision.

I needed to look in greater depth at the original inspection report and see how much progress had been made, why intake numbers were so low, how strong the current finances were and, above all, the implications of the private finance initiative (PFI) debt that the school had incurred in building a new suite of science laboratories.

The original inspection report made disturbing reading. The inspectors had detected an ethos of low expectations, with GCSE outcomes not only significantly below national averages but also below that of similar schools. Less than half of the most able students were making sufficient progress to attain the grades expected of them. There was a gap, on average, of one GCSE grade between the performance of students in receipt of the pupil premium grant and the small minority of students in the academy who were not supported by the grant. Students who were supported at school action plus were making less progress than others nationally in both English and mathematics. While the attainment in some subjects was nearing the national average, too many subjects were not reaching that standard. The quality of teaching was judged to be inadequate, with high levels of teacher absence and a reliance on supply staff being cited as a principal cause. Students' attitudes to learning were judged not to be consistently positive and this was having an impact on their progress. Data systems were not functioning effectively, making it difficult to track student progress and apply appropriate intervention strategies where necessary. Four section 8 visits that followed the 2014 inspection failed to detect any significant improvement. I would need to visit the school to see how much progress had been made since the inspection

The visit confirmed the inspections' findings. Too many pupils were wandering the corridors during lessons. Supply staff were finding it difficult to keep order within the classrooms and there did not seem to be a clear sense of mission or, if there was, I was having difficulty detecting it. The leadership team was working hard but there were too many problems for such a small team to resolve.

The intake of the academy was in decline. I made a point of talking to councillors and community leaders who lived in the area to try to find the reasons behind this decline. The explanation I was given was that the poor academic performance was not seen as attractive to the more aspirant parents and many Muslim parents wanted single-sex education for their daughters. However, this did not seem to become a big concern if they could gain a place at one of the selective, high-performing secondary schools that neighboured the academy. A change of both image and outcomes would be needed if we were to take over the sponsorship.

An investigation of the academy's finances showed that almost £700,000 was being held in reserve. However, these finances would be affected by the significant number of staff who had been suspended and were negotiating compromise agreements. A total of 48 students, including nine in Year 11, were identified as being educated off-site at an annual cost of £185,000. The PFI debt was approximately £700,000 per year and had 17 years still to run. For this payment, the school received full security, caretaking, cleaning, catering, maintenance, insurance and refuse removal, but the cost was non-negotiable and was a considerable strain when student numbers were declining.

I met with the leaders of King's Warrington and The Hawthorne's. We all agreed that taking on such a difficult challenge was a hearts and minds decision. Reason told us that we should walk away but our hearts, consciences and beliefs told us that the students, despite a nucleus of good teachers in the academy, were not getting the overall quality education that they were entitled to as a civic right. With some trepidation, we decided that we would form a multi-academy trust, take the academy on and see if we could use the same strategies that we were using in Warrington and Bootle to turn it around. The original company name for the Warrington project was 'Great Schools for all Children'. We decided to shorten the name and The Great Schools Trust (GST) was founded.

With the Regional Schools Commissioner's help, we were able to develop a cordial relationship with UCAT and they agreed to work with us in ensuring a smooth handover. I was somewhat surprised, but really appreciative, when Michael Taylor told me that he thought the takeover was a really exciting challenge and offered to keep commuting from Hertfordshire for another year and lead both Hawthorne's and the new school. I readily accepted his offer.

Our first challenge was to convince the existing staff that we were not asset strippers but a group of mission-driven people who wanted to turn the academy around as quickly as possible. We used King's Warrington and The Hawthorne's to demonstrate our present track record, but emphasised that we saw education and equality of opportunity as a civil right for all students in the academy. We did not promise anyone an easy time but we did promise them that, if we worked hard together, we would be out of special measures within the next 12 months. At the end of the meeting we received a round of spontaneous applause, which we were certainly not expecting.

Our second challenge was to recruit new staff as soon as possible, as we were determined to be fully staffed by the beginning of the new school year. We took a twin-track approach in solving this challenge. In the first instance we used the Future Leaders and Teach First ambassadors, who presently worked in our two schools, to spread the word that we needed mission-driven people to help us turnaround a failing urban school in really challenging circumstances, especially at leadership level. We then contacted a range of local recruitment agencies and extended an invitation for them to send any interested teachers to an information session at the academy.

We were both surprised and pleased at the number of people who attended the meeting. Our strategy was simple, in that we outlined the plight of the academy's students as well as our determination to lead it out of category within two terms. We stressed that we were not offering any sinecures and were looking for people who would go the extra mile. We were overcome by the positive response to our plea and immediately started to arrange an interview schedule to fill the vacant posts. Within two weeks, Michael was able to appoint a first-class leadership team and, before the term ended, we had appointed sufficiently qualified teachers so as to be fully staffed when the new academy opened in September.

Throughout July, with the help of School Colours, we had measured every student for a new uniform which we were going to pay for out of the academy's financial reserves and worked closely with UCAT in resolving all outstanding suspensions and grievance procedures so that we did not inherit any prolonged disputes. All that seemed to be left to do was the rebranding.

Working with the PFI funders and maintenance contractors, we soon discovered that we could only use their agreed contractors and that we could not use competitive tender to compare prices. We needed the academy fully painted inside and out within the summer vacation and agreed to pay – we would sort out the long-term contract later. We wanted Parker Design to carry out the branding so that all three schools had similar identities. We were told that we would need to pay an additional 15% surcharge to the funders for using a non-agreed contractor, but time was of the essence and we agreed. When the academy opened its doors in September, after an intensive and often fraught six weeks, staff and students walked into a completely refurbished building. Each corridor carried reminders of the ASPIRE Code; inspirational messages surrounded you wherever you went, the now famous 'You too can be...' posters were clearly displayed, and each classroom door carried the name of a university relevant to the subject that was being taught inside. A fresh start was clearly signalled in the new home of King's Leadership Academy Liverpool.

The senior leadership team worked incredibly hard in those first few weeks in showing that the old academy had closed and a new team was in town. From day one, there was an ethos of high expectations and no excuses for poor academic performance. Strict uniform checks happened at the school gates each morning. Assemblies were held to explain the school's beliefs and values, students were trained to line up in tutor or class groups in the school yard, waiting for their teacher to lead them into the next lesson. In order to make the newly imposed system work all staff, including support staff, agreed to line the corridors to encourage a quiet transition. The new social norms were strict but not overly so. On reaching the classroom, hands were shaken and compulsory seating plans gave control of the classroom to the teacher.

In the first few weeks, every student had their reading ability assessed and information from these assessments was used to determine which students should receive additional teaching or further help to develop their skills. The special educational needs co-ordinator completed a full review of pupils to make sure that those with special educational needs had been identified for additional support. Teaching groups were reorganised to allow teachers to better focus on students' additional needs, especially those with very low literacy skills or students who were at an early stage of learning to speak English.

The 39 students who were still being educated off-site were all visited at home. Of these, 13 had settled into the alternative provision and were starting the second year of their GCSE course and had, according to the off-site provider, an attendance of at least 90%. We decided to leave them there at a cost of £55,000. During the summer, an area of the school that had been identified as an internal 'alternative provision unit' was refurbished and named the ASPIRE Centre. Slowly, during the first term, with the help of teachers from the main school who willingly worked in the Centre, we admitted the 39 students previously educated off-site, tranche by tranche. Using the ASPIRE Centre 'half-way house' we eventually reintegrated 26 students back into mainstream school, with many settling back into GCSE courses before the end of the school year.

The data systems were aligned with the other two schools and the learning cycles were introduced so that individual student progress could be measured on a regular basis, as well as the academy's progress in closing the performance gap of differing groups of students.

Teachers from The Hawthorne's readily gave their time to explain the new systems and work alongside their subject colleagues. Lesson observations, work scrutinies and learning cycle outcomes became the focus of the academy's teacher improvement programme. Teachers not reaching the high-expectations standards that were set were put on coaching programmes rather than being given warnings regarding their classroom performance.

The early months were not easy for the staff. A small number of students who had been used to absconding from lessons and meeting under stairwells and in toilets were still trying to test the system but regular corridor patrols were making it very difficult for them. As the term progressed staff morale, confidence and enthusiasm began to rise. A distinct rhythm had been established in the daily life of the school, the school climate was becoming more positive, students were no longer trying to walk out of lessons and a culture of high expectations was slowly emerging.

The academy had inherited the continuation of the monitoring visits and the report from the fifth monitoring visit in December was most positive. In March 2016, the academy received notice of a full inspection just seven months after the change of sponsor. To everyone's delight it was moved out of category. For a second time, we had applied the same educational blueprint as we had used in the 'start-up' free school in Warrington and, once again, it had been successful!

At one of my weekly meetings with Michael Taylor shortly after the inspection he informed me that he thought his work was done. I knew that he thrived on challenges and agreed that, if he could find a new challenge nearer home, the GST would release him from his contract as a way of thanking him for his considerable achievements in leading both schools out of category. In June, Michael found a new challenge in London and I started the search for his replacement.

Reflections on Turning Failing Schools Around

According to the Mass Insight Education and Research Institute a school turnaround is a 'dramatic and comprehensive intervention in a low performing school that produces significant gains in student achievement within two years'. Ofsted would seem to agree with this timeline as schools or academies judged to require special measures, which are not re-brokered, will be subject to a further section 5 inspection no later than 24 months after the first inspection. So, having agreed a timeline we need to ask what is meant by a 'dramatic and comprehensive intervention'? For too long, too many governing bodies or multi-academy trusts have seen this intervention as replacing the headteacher and keeping their fingers crossed. For me, turning a school around is not that simple. The school may need new leadership but without a well-thought-out turnaround plan the new leaders could soon flounder.

Let us start by establishing a few of the benchmarks that a transformation team should be seeking to achieve when turning a school around:

Governance, leadership and accountability
Highly successful schools have a positive school climate and a culture that enables both staff and students to excel. They commit themselves unwaveringly to the setting of high expectations for the conduct of staff and students and focus on consistently improving outcomes for all students, but especially for disadvantaged students. They work hard at maintaining positive relationships between staff and students and are uncompromising in their ambition.

Student attendance, behaviour and motivation

Students in highly successful schools are well motivated and recognise that their attendance is a key priority in achieving their goals. They are confident and self-assured learners with excellent attitudes to learning. These attitudes have a strong, positive impact on their academic progress. There is little, if any, evidence of bullying or prejudice-based behaviour.

The quality of teaching and learning

Highly successful schools have teachers with deep and rich knowledge of the subjects that they teach. Their teachers understand that as well as imparting knowledge they need to encourage, in their students, the development of growth mindsets, high aspirations and the traits of character that will help them succeed. In doing so, they plan their lessons effectively ensuring maximum use of every learning minute. Their plans contain a single, high-level learning objective so that their lessons are pitched high. They are skilled in the use of questioning to not only check understanding and progress but, also, to identify which students will need additional help and support to successfully achieve the high-level objective. They are determined that their students will achieve, and provide both collective and individual incisive feedback as to what their students should do to further improve their knowledge, understanding and skills. They ensure that the enhancement of literacy, oracy and numeracy works exceptionally well within their lessons and manage behaviour successfully, with clear rules that are consistently applied.

Curriculum design

A highly successful school has a curriculum that is broad, balanced and relevant to the starting points and aspirations of the academy's students. It has been designed with the end in mind so that it maximises each student's opportunity to succeed in the external examinations. It offers personalisation and choice at different stages of each student's learning journey and ensures mastery of learning before progression can take place.

Student assessment and reporting procedures

A highly successful school has robust assessment systems which are designed to improve student learning and progress, indicate where intervention may be necessary and keep teachers and parents informed of the progress of individual students.

Student outcomes

A highly successful school will have student outcomes that are above the national average, exceed those of similar schools, show little 'in-school' variation and have minimal gaps in the progress and attainment of differing groups of students.

Parental engagement

A highly successful school has a coherent engagement policy that identifies both formal and informal methods for telling parents and carers about the progress and attitude to learning of their child, as well as engaging them in the daily life of the school.

The Great Schools Trust Turnaround Plan (abridged)

Leadership

1. **Does the present leadership have the capacity to carry out a dramatic and sustainable turnaround plan?**

   Yes: *Retain*

   No: *Consider training or alternative employment in trust*

2. **Is the present leadership mission driven?**

   Yes: *Retain*

   No: *Consider training or alternative employment in trust*

3. **Are there strong and effective accountability structures?**

   Yes*: No action*

   No*: Introduce new line management and accountability structures*

Culture

4. **Is there visible evidence of a culture of high expectations?**

   Yes: *Add GST brand*

   No: *Refurbish and rebrand*

Attendance, behaviour and motivation

5. **Is the academy's attendance for all, and differing groups of, students in line with national expectations?**

   Yes: *No action*

   No: *Introduce GST attendance systems*

6. **Are students' attitude to learning aligned to a culture of high expectations?**

   Yes: *No action*

   No: *Introduce GST attitude to learning systems*

7. **Is student behaviour up to GST expectations?**

   Yes: *No action*

   No: *Introduce GST behaviour systems*

8. **Does the academy have a positive rewards system to increase student motivation?**

   Yes: *No action*

   No: *Introduce GST rewards systems*

Quality of teaching and learning

9. **Are all subjects taught by teachers who are qualified in that subject?**

   Yes: *No action*

   No: *Introduce GST teacher support systems*

10. **Are teachers trained in knowledge plus character teaching methodology?**

    Yes: *No action*

    No: *Introduce GST knowledge-plus training*

11. **Are teachers trained in the encouragement of growth mindsets?**

    Yes: *No action*

    No: *Introduce GST growth mindset training*

12. **Are teachers trained in the development of strong traits of character?**

    Yes: *No action*

    No: *Introduce GST ASPIRE Code training*

13. **Are teachers trained in the 'low workload' planning of lessons?**

    Yes: *No action*

    No: *Introduce GST lesson planning training*

14. **Do teachers see differentiation as providing more support and time rather than lower expectations and weaker knowledge content?**

    Yes: *No action*

    No: *Introduce GST differentiation training*

15. **Do teachers use effective questioning to check individual and collective progress as well as ensuring academic rigour?**

    Yes: *No action*

    No: *Introduce GST 'effective questioning' training*

16. **Are teachers providing effective and meaningful feedback without excess workload?**

    Yes: *No action*

    No: *Introduce GST student feedback training*

17. **Are teachers skilled in effectively enhancing students' literacy, oracy and numeracy in their lessons?**

    Yes: *No action*

    No: *Introduce GST 'access skills' training*

18. **Do any teachers need help in improving their behaviour management skills?**

    Yes: *Introduce GST behaviour management skill training to identified individuals*

    No: *No action*

19. **Do school leaders have sufficient skills to monitor the quality of teaching against the required standards?**

    Yes: *No action*

    No: *Individual lesson observation training to identified individuals*

20. **Do school leaders have sufficient skills to coach teachers to the required standards?**

    Yes: *No action*

    No: *Individual coaching training to identified individuals*

21. **Do school leaders have sufficient skills to deal sensitively with teachers who, despite intensive coaching, fail to reach the required standards?**

    Yes: *No action*

    No: *Individual coaching training to identified individuals*

Curriculum Design

22. **Does the academy use CAT tests prior to entry to establish individual, personalised entry plans for all students?**

    Yes: *No action*

    No: *Introduction of Saturday Assessment Morning shortly after SAT tests in Year 6*

23. **Does the academy's present curriculum emphasise literacy, oracy and numeracy to GST standards, ensure mastery before progression, address cultural and character deficits in students and maximise each students opportunities to succeed in external examinations?**

    Yes: *No action*

    No: *GST curriculum design training for senior leaders*

Student assessment and reporting procedures

24. **Are the academy's assessment procedures robust enough to detect underachievement?**

    Yes: *Align with GST assessment systems*

    No: *Introduce GST assessment systems*

25. **Does the academy have an effective system of setting progress targets for all students?**

    Yes: *No action*

    No: *Import GST target setting practices*

26. **Does the academy assess its students five times each year?**

    Yes: *No action*

    No: *Import GST Learning Cycle, assessment and intervention practices*

27. **Does the academy send reports home five times each year?**

    Yes: *No action*

    No: *Import GST 'reporting to parents' practices*

Student Outcomes

28. **Does the academy have effective strategies for maximising student outcomes, reducing in-school variation and minimising the progress and attainment of differing groups of students?**

    Yes: *No action*

    No: *Import GST raising achievement strategies*

Parental engagement

29. **Does the academy's parental engagement meet GST standards?**

    Yes: *No action*

    No: *Import GST parental engagement strategies*

As well as having a plan, every transformation team should have a thorough understanding of the change management process and why it often fails. Let's start with the failure side. Most change fails because those leading the change process concentrate on introducing new strategies, systems and practices and not the people in the organisation. Change is really about people. You may put in new systems and practices but if the people who have to use them don't buy into them, then you will find that they soon drift back to their old ways. Change management is about winning over the hearts and minds of the people involved in the change so that they see the benefit of the change and work hard with you to make it succeed.

An Eight-Step Model for Effective Change

1. *Audit your present position to see what needs to change.*
2. *Create a strong vision of what success will look like.*
3. *Build a convincing case as to why change is necessary.*
4. *Develop a strategic plan to implement the change.*
5. *Plan milestones and success criteria.*
6. *Communicate your vision in as many different ways as you can, remembering that you need to win the hearts and minds of those who need to work within the changed organisation.*
7. *Ensure quick wins and celebrate them.*
8. *Embed the change.*

2016–17:
Generosity of Spirit

Some months before Michael Taylor resigned, I met with the GST's board of directors to look at succession planning so that his departure would not affect the progress that the two schools were making. We decided that we had developed a distinctive educational model that was working successfully in all three schools and that we did not want to appoint new principals who would want to change the model. It became a policy that, in the first instance, all senior posts would be advertised across the GST before a national advert was considered.

Mark O'Hagan was the deputy principal at King's Leadership Academy Liverpool. He had been an incredible find when we took over the academy. He was 'Future Leader' trained and had been a deputy headteacher at a local school. He lived in the neighbourhood and had a good understanding of its challenges. Peter Gaul was one of two deputy principals at The Hawthorne's. He was a former member of the leadership team of St. Wilfred's, which was one of the schools from which the free school had been formed and had worked in Bootle for many years. Both Peter and Mark were excellent leaders, teachers and team builders and, fortunately for the GST, they applied for the vacant principal's post in their own school. Both interviewed extremely well, laying out detailed plans of how they wanted to build on the emerging success of the schools by placing greater emphasis on the ASPIRE Code and bringing in many of the successful practices that had been honed in Warrington, as well as some well thought-out initiatives of their own. Both were unanimously appointed by the board to lead their schools in June 2015. Michael Taylor's brief had been to lead both schools out of category. Now, we needed to bring the three schools closer together in strengthening the trust model in all three schools. Shane and Andrew, from King's Warrington, immediately contacted both of the successful applicants, offering their congratulations as well as any help or resources that they might need in bringing their schools' organisational model closer to that of Warrington.

In September 2013, Ofsted had published a report on Key Stage 3 in English secondary schools called 'The wasted years'. The executive summary of the report stated:

> *'Leaders of successful schools set the right culture for learning that is embraced by their pupils from the outset. They ensure that pupils are well aware of their school's high expectations for behaviour and conduct, and they have a clear understanding of pupils' achievements in primary school and build on them from day one. These leaders ensure that their schools embed the learning habits that will stand their pupils in good stead for their future academic studies, for example in stressing the importance of reading often and widely.'*

As a trust, we had already made a lot of progress in this direction. Warrington had a well-defined 'school culture' induction programme for all of their Year 7 students which was based on a high-expectations philosophy, the ASPIRE Code and the tie ceremony. They readily provided Peter and Mark with both human and physical resources to adjust the programme to the educational starting points of their own schools' intake. Using the Warrington experience, cognitive ability testing was introduced in both schools to produce trust-wide baselines against which improvement targets could be set. Common reading analysis tests were introduced across the trust and, in both The Hawthorne's and King's Liverpool, greater emphasis was placed on improving literacy, oracy and numeracy with the longer term ambition of starting each day with silent reading on arrival at school to stress the importance of reading often and widely. Trust-wide organisational structures were aligned with all three schools adopting a foundations and senior school approach.

'The wasted years' report also commented that:

> *'The status of Key Stage 3 as the poor relation to other key stages was exemplified in the way schools monitored and assessed pupils' progress.'*

All three schools had excellent monitoring systems for monitoring progress in Years 7 and 8 but were fully aware that, unlike senior school students who had the external examinations to focus on, there was not the same focus available to students in foundations. Working together, all three schools set about providing a sharper focus for foundations through the introduction of an FCBacc – Foundations Character Baccalaureate – in each of the schools. The structure of the qualification would be the same in all three schools, with emphasis on attendance and punctuality, attitude to learning, improved reading and mathematical age, public speaking, residential and public service experience. Each school would have the freedom to determine their own approach and graduating targets. The only trust-wide stipulation would be the introduction of a formal graduation ceremony at the end of Year 8, with full pomp including students wearing gowns to graduate. We were determined that by working together foundations would not be seen as 'wasted years' in any trust school.

Both Mark and Peter decided to place much greater emphasis on the ASPIRE Code in their respective schools. King's Liverpool had had sufficient funding to have a full ASPIRE rebrand, but The Hawthorne's was not in such a lucky position. Despite the lack of funding, Peter and his team invested heavily in time to produce ASPIRE posters and symbols around the school during summer break before his first full year as principal began. While Warrington had already introduced a 'monarch' system of rewards for behaviours that best reflected the ASPIRE Code neither of the other two schools had followed that path. Working with Scott Cordon, his newly appointed vice principal, Mark invested in an electronically-based rewards scheme called Epraise with a 'points means prizes' approach to embedding behaviours in accord with the ASPIRE Code. Peter decided to follow the Urban Prep approach and ordered ASPIRE ties to be awarded each week to students who best modelled the Code. All three schools now make regular use of the Brathay Trust for outdoor leadership experience in both Years 7 and 8 and the Duke of Edinburgh's Award is beginning to emerge in the first year of their senior school.

All academy leaders were keen to provide a greater vehicle for student voice in their schools. Shane and Andy provided the other two schools with the organisational structure of Warrington's student parliament so that each of the other schools could not only have their own student parliaments but, also, that we would all work together to produce a trust-wide student parliament.

Andy Reay was keen to expand the combined cadet force (CCF) into all three academies to reinforce the 'character through leadership' programme and held endless meetings with officials at the Ministry of Defence (MoD) to gain permission and financial support. He was extremely successful and gained funding to appoint James Hudson, an experienced cadet force leader, to work across the GST, as well as introducing an air cadets' corps into King's Liverpool and a marine cadets' corps into The Hawthorne's. A MoD requirement was that each school had to schedule a two-hour session each week as 'parade time' so that sufficient time was scheduled for the initiative to become embedded in the culture of both schools. In April 2018, the GST is scheduled to bring the officers and cadets of all three schools together for its first parade day and regimental dinner which, hopefully, will become yet another trust-wide initiative.

The introduction of parade time resulted in a change of school day in both King's Liverpool and The Hawthorne's. King's Liverpool had extended Monday afternoon by one lesson and The Hawthorne's had extended Thursday afternoon in a similar fashion. With Warrington's parade day being Wednesday afternoon this allowed CCF staff, all on central contracts, to work across the three schools. To accommodate the extended afternoon, all three schools now finish early on a Friday for weekly professional development sessions.

Moving away from five days per year to weekly sessions made 'continuous' a reality in terms of the GST's teacher-based continuous professional development programmes. This now allows the GST to bring lead practitioners and subject teams together at least once during each learning cycle. To ensure that end of learning cycle assessments are accurate, the three schools have become engaged in cross-trust moderation at the end of each cycle and have further extended this practice to include the three 'pre-public examinations' practices that are held in Year 11, so that the students have no fear of the final examinations. Regular cross-trust meetings and shared training days have led to the stronger departments in the GST helping those who wish to improve. Resources, both human and physical, are being shared and common schemes of work and lesson plans are being produced with the intent of easing teacher workload.

To improve student outcomes, both King's Liverpool and The Hawthorne's extended their school day for Year 11, aligning with King's Warrington, and organised what is now known as the 'Period 6 Revision Programme'. These very well-attended sessions are meant to stop Year 11 teachers giving up well-deserved and needed holidays to hold revision classes. Unfortunately many of our dedicated teachers have ignored this attempt to ease their workload and still use period six and the holidays to further tutor Year 11 students, but we are working on it.

To give their teachers and students greater insight into the new GCSEs, King's Liverpool organised a series of 'examiners' conferences' for both teachers and students. Again, demonstrating great spirit of generosity, they have opened these conferences to all three schools with the intent of them becoming a trust-wide annual event.

Mark and Peter are firm advocates of community involvement as a way of re-engaging disengaged urban families and, independently of each other, had started their own community programmes. In Liverpool, Mark and his team had opened a Saturday morning school to offer their students somewhere to go at the weekend, as well as holiday clubs each school break and a well-attended community fair in early summer. Peter's team had introduced ASPIRE Sports as their vehicle for after-school and Saturday student involvement and had also introduced holiday plays schemes each school break, as well as an autumn fair and a Halloween Special.

In the previous year Shane had interviewed for a head of music for the Warrington school. Although he did not appoint her, he was very impressed with the candidate who came second and suggested to Mark and Peter that not only might she fill the part-time music vacancies in their schools, but she could become choral leader for all three schools, with the eventual aim of producing a trust-wide choir. Seeing the advantages of such an appointment they readily agreed and the GST is now seeing the emergence of not only a GST choir but also a GST samba band!

The Hawthorne's English department had been organising 'Shakespeare by Heart' days as part of a school-wide approach to public speaking. Showing the same spirit of generosity as many others in the GST, this was opened up to all three schools and a shield awarded annually to the winning school.

Alongside these joint activities all three school have launched a series of initiatives of their own. King's Liverpool serves a very diverse area and has introduced immersion and extraction strategies for the significant number of students who arrive without any English at all, as well as parental-engagement strategies that translates all messages into the home language of each English as an additional language student. The school has just about found sufficient finance to further emulate King's Warrington by supplying all Year 7 students with Chromebooks, with the intention of spreading this initiative across the whole school over the next five years.

The Hawthorne's have learned from King's Liverpool and have introduced their own version of the ASPIRE Centre called the 'school within a school', so as to move towards a trust objective of having no permanent or temporary exclusions and avoiding the 'pass the parcel' that too many schools adopt with their most challenging students.

All three schools now have strong and extensive links with higher education so as to further raise the aspirations of their students.

The GST was only formed in November 2015 and, in the two years that have followed, we have moved, at many levels, from three individual schools to one trust, firmly focused on its mission of breaking glass ceilings to enhance the social mobility of our students.

This would not have happened without a great display of an incredible spirit of generosity at so many levels and great leadership in each school. These two factors made my role as its first CEO much easier.

Reflections on the Role of the CEO

I have been the CEO of the GST since it was formed in 2015. In that time I have found it to be a fascinating role, in that it combines vision with delivery, shared responsibility alongside accountability, challenge with accompanying support and the ability to work at both local and national level at the same time. What I have discovered in those two years is that the ideal CEO is a very friendly version of Cerberus, the three-headed mythical watchdog of the Greek underworld, who was charged with minding the gates of hell. Multi-academy trusts are far from hell but, for me, a good CEO has to have three heads that work both independently and collectively. One head is always outward-looking, the second head is continually inward-looking, while the third head is forward-looking and firmly concentrated on the future.

The outward-looking responsibilities
- **The guardian of the flame** *in that the CEO is the fierce protector of the Trust's beliefs, values, mission, vision and reputation.*
- **The ambassador** *who is the public face or representative of the Trust.*
- **The communicator** *who continually spreads the good news regarding the achievements of the Trust.*
- **The champion** *of all of the Trusts' successes.*

The inward-looking responsibilities
- **The conductor of the orchestra** *in that the CEO sets the tempo for the Trust, bringing the musicians of several different orchestras together in harmony as they seek perfection.*

- **The praetorian guard** *of the Trust's climate and culture.*
- **The thinker and strategist** *who analyses trends and thinks of new strategies.*
- **The performance analyst** *who analyses performance and provides objective feedback.*
- **The financial analyst** *who is continually analysing the financial status of the Trust, ensuring that it is sound.*
- **The provider of resources** *who will always find the resources to support a good idea.*
- **The plate spinner** *who hurries up and down the stage ensuring all of the plates keep spinning and none fall over.*
- **The searcher** *who continually seeks good practice and transfers it to where it is needed.*
- **The mentor** *who supports the growth of others by passing on acquired knowledge and wisdom.*
- **The coach** *who works closely with others, helping improve their performance.*
- **The guru** *who acts as a teacher, guide or adviser in times of need.*
- **The teaching and learning guardian** *who ensures the highest quality of teaching and learning in every classroom, every day.*
- **The quality assurer** *who ensures the highest possible quality in all aspects of the work of the Trust.*

The forward-looking responsibilities

- **The futurist** *who peers into crystal balls and looks over hills to keep the Trust one step ahead.*
- **The weather forecaster** *who detects how the wind is changing long before it changes.*
- **The leadership developer** *who continually tends and grows leaders for the future development of the Trust.*

2017:
Breaking Glass Ceilings

Within the Trust, what is now known as the 'GST Aspirational Model' is still in its infancy in both The Hawthorne's and King's Leadership Academy Liverpool, who both serve incredibly challenging communities. King's Warrington, a non-selective school, has been carefully implementing, nurturing and developing the model for five years.

Despite being an 11–16 school, staff at The Hawthorne's have been closely monitoring the number of their Year 11 students who are not only entering sixth form college but successfully applying for university. In 2016, four years after the school opened, six students entered university – all of them being the first in their family. In 2017 this number had risen to 20 – again, all but one were first timers! Unfortunately, with the introduction of the new examination system GCSE outcomes have, for the first time, taken a slight dip. Far too many of the English papers have had to be remarked, with one coming back 14 marks higher. Such an error, if left undetected, can ruin the opportunities of a student and, in such a small school, can cost 2.5% in the published tables.

King's Liverpool has taken an added approach to monitoring students through local sixth forms. Working with the Springboard Charity, the school has been successful in applying for bursary grants to enable its students to enter the sixth form of an independent school. In 2017, they had their first success and, at the time of writing, five Year 11 students have been offered free bursaries to enter the sixth forms of successful independent schools, subject to G.C.S.E. outcomes, including one offer from Eton College! GCSE outcomes rose dramatically in

2017 and, with the school's Progress 8 score being recorded as '-0.13', it has been recognised as Liverpool's most improved school.

The Year 11 students in Warrington have, after five years of constantly applying the model, achieved incredible outcomes with 93% of their students passing English and mathematics at Level 4 or above, 65% passing at Level 5 or above, 51% achieving an EBacc, a Progress 8 score of 0.27 and 95% entering post-16 education!

The staff of all three schools have worked tirelessly in implementing the GST model and I am confident that, in years to come, their students will not just break glass ceilings but dismantle them for good.

Reflections on the Principal Drivers of an 'Enhanced Social Mobility' focused School

This book started with me, sipping coffee at a Starbucks in O'Hare Airport, wondering if I had actually used the right approaches in leading two urban schools. When I first became a headteacher in 1980 I was very child-centred in my approaches. By 2004, when I gave up headship, I had changed the way I led schools. I often wonder what brought about these gradual changes and the only reasons I can think of are the influences of Ofsted inspections and the publication of league tables. I was wrong to be so child-centred, as I was thinking short term and not long term regarding the lives of the young people in my school, but I may have been equally wrong by 2004 when, as with so many other school leaders, I thought of the overall school performance before listening to my inner conscience and thinking about the future life prospects of the young people in my school.

The publication of league tables and the ranking of schools has, in my humble opinion, led to a gaming and checklist approach to our noble profession. Perhaps it is time to change the education world. How can we do this?

- *Place a firm emphasis on the beliefs, values, mission and vision of our schools.*
- *Make these values living rather than laminated by establishing them as the lingua franca of the school.*

- *Work hard at establishing a positive school climate that encourages all young people to want to come to school.*

- *Nurture a high-expectations culture within the school, encouraging aspiration and igniting the fires of ambition in our young people.*

- *Constantly expose our young people to positive role models who have made full use of their education.*

- *Change our approaches to differentiation by pitching our lesson objectives high and using additional support and added time as our differentiator in helping all young people succeed at the highest levels.*

- *Use a 'teach–assess–remediate' approach to learning by establishing learning cycles.*

- *Use data forensically to rectify gaps in knowledge and skills so that we remediate rather than grade.*

- *Accept that teaching is not just about passing knowledge from generation to generation, as important as that is, but about developing in our young people such character strengths as determination, resilience and perseverance so that they do not give up before success happens.*

- *Bring academic rigour back in to all of our classrooms.*

- *Ensure we address intellectual, social and cultural imbalances by broadening our curriculum offer through well planned visits to universities, museums, art galleries, theatres, concerts, and so on.*

This is a long and ambitious list but is easily achievable by a mission-driven leader.

2018: What next?

2018 will be the year of my 75th birthday. By September of 2018, I will have been involved in state education for 53 years. During that time I have been a teacher, a school leader, a coach and a CEO. People often ask me which was the most rewarding of these roles and it is a difficult question to answer. They were all richly rewarding. What I do know is that the last 12 years have not only been really exciting, but have flown by.

This story started in 2006 when I was given the opportunity to undertake a four-year study of charter school successes in the most challenging areas of such cities as New York, Boston and Chicago. It was on the downtown streets of Chicago that I gained the inspiration to try to bring the best of ideas together and hopefully form a new educational paradigm. Since 2012, I have been lucky enough to work alongside some great people in the North-West of England in implementing this new approach in three schools. Each school has a strong sense of moral purpose and are driven by strong values. Each has a strong focus on increasing the intellectual, social and cultural capital of its students and 'knowledge plus character' teaching is practised in the classrooms of all three schools. The schools are mission driven in that they are determined to harness the power of knowledge acquisition, character enhancement and leadership development to give each of their young students the aspiration and strength of character to fulfil their true potential and compete with their more advantaged peers on a level playing field.

If you have ever received an email from me you might have noticed, just below the signature line, a quote from Margaret Mead, an American anthropologist. It reads:

> *'Never doubt that a small group of thoughtful, committed, citizens can change the world. Indeed, it is the only thing that ever has.'*

I stumbled upon this quote more than 20 years ago and it is the power of her words that continually drive me forward. Three schools is not a large-scale revolution, but we hope that our achievements will encourage others to join us in our mission to produce a fairer society where all young people have the same equality of educational opportunity and glass ceilings no longer exist. By adopting Margaret Mead's words as our mantra, we can change the world of education and ensure that the doors to bright futures are open to all young people, irrespective of their postcode or financial status.

And what of my future? People often ask me when I intend to retire. My answer is always 'soon'… unless another challenge comes over the horizon.